Succeed on the Standardized Test

This Book Includes:

- 2 Performance Based Assessments (PBA)
- 2 End-Of-Year (EOY) Assessments
- Detailed Answer explanations for every question
- Type I questions - Concepts, Skills and Procedures
  Type II questions - Expressing Mathematical Reasoning
  Type III questions - Modeling and/or Applications
- Strategies for building speed and accuracy
- Content aligned with the new Common Core State Standards

Plus access to Online Workbooks which include:

- Hundreds of practice questions
- Self-paced learning and personalized score reports
- Instant feedback after completion of the workbook

Complement Classroom Learning All Year

Using the Lumos Study Program, parents and teachers can reinforce the classroom learning experience for children. It creates a collaborative learning platform for students, teachers and parents.

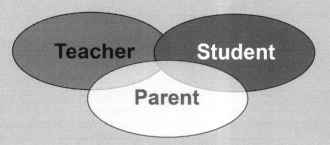

Used in Schools and Public Libraries To Improve Student Achievement

Lumos Learning

Common Core Assessments and Online Workbooks: Grade 8 Mathematics, PARCC Edition

Contributing Editor - Eric Ibsen-Johnson
Contributing Editor - Gregory Applegate
Curriculum Director - Marisa Adams
Executive Producer - Mukunda Krishnaswamy
Illustrator & Designer - Raghavendra Rao R.

ISBN-10: 1940484235

ISBN-13: 978-1-940484-23-5

Printed in the United States of America

For permissions and additional information contact us

Lumos Information Services, LLC
PO Box 1575, Piscataway, NJ 08855-1575
http://www.LumosLearning.com

Email: support@lumoslearning.com
Tel: (732) 384-0146
Fax: (866) 283-6471

Lumos Learning

Table of Contents

Introduction

The Common Core State Standards Initiative (CCSS) was created from the need to have more robust and rigorous guidelines, which could be standardized from state to state. These guidelines create a learning environment where students will be able to graduate high school with all skills necessary to be active and successful members of society, whether they take a role in the workforce or in some sort of post-secondary education.

Once the CCSS were fully developed and implemented, it became necessary to devise a way to ensure they were assessed appropriately. To this end, states adopting the CCSS have joined one of two consortia, either PARCC or Smarter Balanced.

What is PARCC?

The Partnership for Assessment of Readiness for College and Careers (PARCC) is one of the two state consortiums responsible for developing assessments aligned to the new, more rigorous Common Core State Standards. A combination of educational leaders from PARCC Governing and Participating states, along with test developers, have worked together to create the new computer based English Language Arts and Math Assessments.

PARCC has spent the better part of two years developing their new assessments, and in many ways, they will be unlike anything many students have ever seen. The tests will be conducted online, requiring students to complete tasks to assess a deeper understanding of the CCSS. Additionally, instead of one final test at the end of the year, PARCC understands that the best way to measure student success is to assess them multiple times a year. So, students in PARCC states will take a mid-year assessment called a Performance Based Assessment (PBA) and an End-of-Year Assessment (EOY).

How Can the Lumos Study Program Prepare Students for PARCC Tests?

Beginning in the fall of 2014, student mastery of Common Core State Standards will be assessed using standardized testing methods. At Lumos Learning, we believe that year-long learning and adequate practice before the actual test are the keys to success on these standardized tests. We have designed the Lumos study program to help students get plenty of realistic practice before the test and to promote year long collaborative learning.

This is a Lumos **tedBook**™. It connects you to Online Workbooks and additional resources using a number of devices including Android phones, iPhones, tablets and personal computers. The Lumos StepUp Online Workbooks are designed to promote year-long learning. It is a simple program students can securely access using a computer or device with internet access. It consists of hundreds of grade appropriate questions, aligned to the new Common Core State Standards. Students will get instant feedback and can review their answers anytime. Each student's answers and progress can be reviewed by parents and educators to reinforce the learning experience.

How to use this book effectively

The Lumos Program is a flexible learning tool. It can be adapted to suit a student's skill level and the time available to practice before standardized tests. Here are some tips to help you use this book and the online workbooks effectively:

Students
- Take one Performance Based Assessment (PBA).
- Use the "Related Lumos StepUp™ Online Workbook" in the Answer Key section to identify the topic that is related to each question.
- Use the Online workbooks to practice your areas of difficulty and complement classroom learning.
- Download the Lumos StepUp™ app using the instructions provided in Lumos StepUp™ Mobile App FAQ to have anywhere access to online resources.
- Have open-ended questions evaluated by a teacher or parent, keeping in mind the scoring rubrics.
- Take the second PBA as you get close to the test date.
- Complete the test in a quiet place, following the test guidelines. Practice tests provide you an opportunity to improve your test-taking skills and to review topics included in the PARCC test.
- As the end of the year becomes closer, take one EOY and follow the above guidelines before taking the second.

Parents
- Familiarize yourself with the PARCC test format and expectations.
- Help your child use Lumos StepUp™ Online Workbooks by following the instructions in "How to access the Lumos Online Workbooks" section of this chapter.
- Download the Lumos SchoolUp™ app using the instructions provided in the Lumos SchoolUp™ Mobile App FAQ section of this chapter to get useful school information.
- Review your child's performance in the "Lumos Online Workbooks" periodically. You can do this by simply asking your child to log into the system online and select the subject area you wish to review.
- Review your child's work in the practice PBA's and EOY's.

Teachers
- Please contact **support@lumoslearning.com** to request a **teacher account.** A teacher account will help you create custom assessments and lessons as well as review the online work of your students. Visit **http://www.lumoslearning.com/math-quill** to learn more.
- Download the Lumos SchoolUp™ app using the instructions provided in Lumos SchoolUp™ Mobile App FAQ to get convenient access to Common Core State Standards and additional school related resources.
- If your school has purchased the school edition of this book, please use this book as the Teacher Guide.
- You can use the Lumos online programs along with this book to complement and extend your classroom instruction.

PARCC Frequently Asked Questions

What Will PARCC Math Assessment Look Like?

For Math, PARCC differentiates three different types of questions:

Type I – Tasks assessing concepts, skills, procedures (Machine scorable only)
- Balance of conceptual understanding, fluency, and application
- Can involve any or all mathematical practice standards
- Machine scorable including innovative, computer-based formats
- Will appear on the End of Year and Performance Based Assessment components

Type II - Tasks assessing expressing mathematical reasoning
- Each task calls for written arguments/justifications, critique of reasoning or precision in mathematical statements (MP.3, 6).
- Can involve other mathematical practice standards
- May include a mix of machine-scored and hand-scored responses
- Included on the Performance Based Assessment component

Type III - Tasks assessing modeling/applications
- Each task calls for modeling/application in a real-world context or scenario (MP.4)
- Can involve other mathematical practice standards
- May include a mix of machine-scored and hand-scored responses
- Included on the Performance Based Assessment component

The PBA will be administered once 75% of the school year is complete. It will consist of Type I, Type II, and Type III questions. In the PBA, students will be given a set amount of time to complete their tasks.

The time for each PBA is described below:

Estimated Time on Task in Minutes (PBA)		
Grade	Session One	Session Two
3	50	50
4	50	50
5	50	50
6	50	50
7	50	50
8	50	50

 © Lumos Information Services 2014   LumosLearning.com

The EOY will be administered once 90% of the school year is complete. It will consist of Type I questions only. In the EOY, students will also be given a set amount of time to complete their tasks.

The time for each EOY is described below:

Estimated Time on Task in Minutes (EOY)		
Grade	Session One	Session Two
3	55	55
4	55	55
5	55	55
6	55	55
7	55	55
8	55	55

What is a PARCC Aligned Test Practice Book?

Inside this book, you will find four full-length practice tests that are similar to the standardized tests students will take to assess their mastery of CCSS-aligned curriculum. Completing these tests will help students master the different areas that are included in newly aligned standardized tests and practice test taking skills. The results will help the students and educators get insights into students' strengths and weaknesses in specific content areas. These insights could be used to help students strengthen their skills in difficult topics and to improve speed and accuracy while taking the test.

How is this Lumos tedBook aligned to PARCC Guidelines?

Although the PARCC assessments will be conducted online, the practice tests here have been created to accurately reflect the depth and rigor of PARCC tasks in a pencil and paper format. Students will still be exposed to the Technology Enhanced Constructed-Response (TECR) style questions so they become familiar with the wording and how to think through these types of tasks.

This edition of the practice test book was created in the Summer 2014 and aligned to the most current PARCC standards released to date. Some changes will occur as PARCC continues to release new information in the fall of 2014 and beyond.

Where can I get more information about PARCC?

You can obtain up-to-date information on PARCC, including sample assessment items, schedules, & the answers to frequently asked questions from the PARCC website at **http://www.parcconline.org**

Where can I get additional information about the Common Core State Standards (CCSS)?

Please visit **http://www.corestandards.org/Math**

How to access the Lumos Online Workbooks

First Time Access:

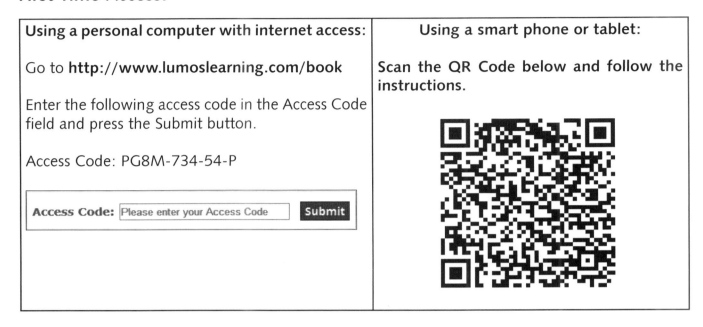

Using a personal computer with internet access:	Using a smart phone or tablet:
Go to **http://www.lumoslearning.com/book** Enter the following access code in the Access Code field and press the Submit button. Access Code: PG8M-734-54-P Access Code: [Please enter your Access Code] Submit	Scan the QR Code below and follow the instructions.

In the next screen, click on the "New User" button to register your user name and password.

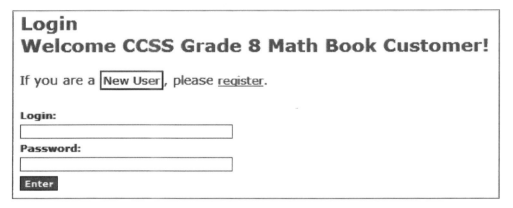

Login
Welcome CCSS Grade 8 Math Book Customer!

If you are a [New User], please register.

Login:
[   ]
Password:
[   ]
Enter

Subsequent Access:

After you establish your user id and password for subsequent access, simply login with your account information.

What if I buy more than one Lumos Study Program?
Please note that you can use all Online Workbooks with one User ID and Password. If you buy more than one book, you will access them with the same account.

Go back to the **http://www.lumoslearning.com/book** link and enter the access code provided in the second book. In the next screen simply login using your previously created account.

     LumosLearning.com

Lumos StepUp™ Mobile App FAQ For Students

What is the Lumos StepUp™ App?

It is a FREE application you can download onto your Android smart phones, tablets, iPhones, and iPads.

What are the Benefits of the StepUp™ App?

This mobile application gives convenient access to Common Core State Standards, Practice Tests, Online Workbooks, and learning resources through your smart phone and tablet computers.

Do I Need the StepUp™ App to Access Online Workbooks?

No, you can access Lumos StepUp™ Online Workbooks through a personal computer. The StepUp™ app simply enhances your learning experience and allows you to conveniently access StepUp™ Online Workbooks and additional resources through your smart phone or tablet.

How can I Download the App?

Visit **lumoslearning.com/a/stepup-app** using your smart phone or tablet and follow the instructions to download the app.

**QR Code
for Smart Phone
Or Tablet Users**

Lumos SchoolUp™ Mobile App FAQ For Parents

What is the Lumos SchoolUp™ App?

It is a FREE App that helps parents and teachers get a wide range of useful information about their school. It can be downloaded onto smartphones and tablets from popular App Stores.

What are the Benefits of the Lumos SchoolUp™ App?

It provides convenient access to
- School performance reports.
- School "Stickies". A Sticky could be information about an upcoming test, homework, extra curricular activities and other school events. Parents and educators can easily create their own sticky and share with the school community.
- Common Core State Standards.
- Sample questions.
- Educational blogs.
- StepUp™ student activity reports.

How can I Download the App?

Visit **lumoslearning.com/a/schoolup-app** using your smartphone or tablet and follow the instructions provided to download the App. Alternatively, scan the QR Code provided below using your smartphone or tablet computer.

QR Code
for Smart Phone
Or Tablet Users

Is SchoolUp™ available for Apple Devices?

SchoolUp™ will be available for Apple devices in the future. The initial release is supported on the Android platform. However, users with iPhones or iPads can use the web version of SchoolUp™ by logging on to **lumoslearning.com/a/schoolup**

Test Taking Tips

1) **The day before the test, make sure you get a good night's sleep.**

2) **On the day of the test, be sure to eat a good hearty breakfast! Also, be sure to arrive at school on time.**

3) **During the test:**

- **Read every question carefully.**

  - Do not spend too much time on any one question. Work steadily through all questions in the section.
  - Attempt all of the questions even if you are not sure of some answers.
  - If you run into a difficult question, eliminate as many choices as you can and then pick the best one from the remaining choices. Intelligent guessing will help you increase your score.
  - Also, mark the question so that if you have extra time, you can return to it after you reach the end of the section. Try to erase the marks after you complete the work.
  - Some questions may refer to a graph, chart, or other kind of picture. Carefully review the graphic before answering the question.
  - Be sure to include explanations for your written responses and show all work.

- **While Answering Multiple-Choice (EBSR) questions.**

  - Completely fill in the bubble corresponding to your answer choice.
  - Read all of the answer choices, even if think you have found the correct answer.

- **While Answering TECR questions.**

  - Read the directions of each question. Some might ask you to drag something, others to select, and still others to highlight. Follow all instructions of the question (or questions if it is in multiple parts)

Performance Based Assessment (PBA) - 1

Student Name: **Start Time:**
Test Date: **End Time:**

Here are some reminders for when you are taking the Grade 8 Mathematics Performance Based Assessment (PBA).

To answer the questions on the test, use the directions given in the question. If you do not know the answer to a question, skip it and go on to the next question. If time permits, you may return to questions in this session only. Do your best to answer every question.

---

1. **PART A**

   Triangle ABC has side lengths of 7, 24, and 25. Is this a right triangle?

   PART B

   In the box below, explain and justify your answer.

   PART C

   Using the same reasoning as above, find the missing length of triangle EFG that would make it a right triangle if leg $\overline{EF}$ is 8 and hypotenuse $\overline{FG}$ is 17.

LumosLearning.com

2.   Tyrell has a total of 15 dimes and nickels in his pocket. The total value of the coins is $1.15. How many dimes and nickels does he have?

Explain how you arrived at your answer.

```

```

3.   **PART A**

A car and bus are both traveling from Houston, TX, to San Antonio, TX. The car is traveling at a rate of 75 mph, while the bus is traveling at a rate of 60 mph. Graph the rate of each vehicle on the graph below. Then, write a statement in the box below that describes the rate shown in the graph.

```

```

PART B

If San Antonio is 185 miles from Houston, how long will it take the bus and the car to make the trip?

```

```

PART C

Suppose the bus leaves $1\frac{1}{4}$ hours before the car. Who will reach San Antonio first?

PART D

Explain your answer to part C.

4. ## PART A

Jorge is filling a cylindrical container with water. If it has a diameter of 3 in. and a height of 5 in., how much water will it hold in terms of π?

PART B

Marisa has an ice cream cone with the same measurements as Jorge. If she fills up her cone exactly to the top without going over, what is the volume of the ice cream in her cone, in terms of π?

PART C

What is the relationship between the volume of the cylinder and the volume of the cone?

5.   Which of the following choices demonstrates the converse of the Pythagorean theorem?

    Ⓐ If $a^2 + c^2 = b^2$, it's a right triangle
    Ⓑ If $c^2 + b^2 = a^2$, it's a right triangle
    Ⓒ If $a^2 + b^2 = c^2$, it's a right triangle
    Ⓓ None of the above.

6.   Triangle ABC has coordinates of A (2, 9), B (2, 5), and C (5, 5) Triangle ADE has coordinates of A (2, 9), D (2, 1), and E (8, 1) as shown below in the graph:

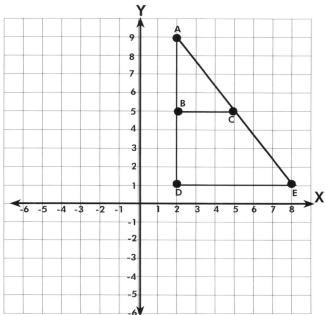

PART A

What is the slope of $\overline{AC}$?

Ⓐ $-\dfrac{3}{4}$

Ⓑ $\dfrac{3}{4}$

Ⓒ $\dfrac{4}{3}$

Ⓓ $-\dfrac{4}{3}$

PART B

What is the slope of $\overline{AE}$?

Ⓐ $\dfrac{4}{3}$

Ⓑ $\dfrac{3}{4}$

Ⓒ $-\dfrac{4}{3}$

Ⓓ $-\dfrac{3}{4}$

PART C

Comparing all sides of the triangles, what statement can be made?

Ⓐ △ABC ≅ △ADE
Ⓑ △ABC ∼ △ADE
Ⓒ △ABC ∼ △AED
Ⓓ △ABC = △ADE

7. ## PART A

Create 2 tables. One table follows the function f(s) = s². The other table follows the function f(s) = 4s. Start at 0 and use whole number values including 5.

PART B

Graph both functions below.

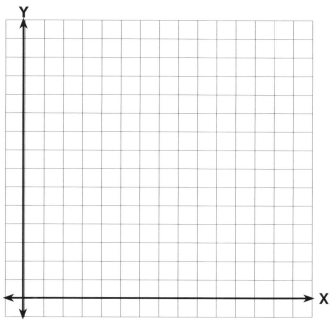

PART C

Describe both graphs in how they are similar and how they are different.

8. John buys 3 shirts and 4 pairs of pants for $133.85. At the same time, Jim is shopping in the same store. He buys 4 shirts and 3 pairs of pants. He spends $127.95. Set up and solve a system of equations that will determine how much one shirt and one pair of pants are.

9.   <u>**PART A**</u>

Graph the following system of equations and identify the solution:
4x – y = 2 and 3x – 2y = 6.

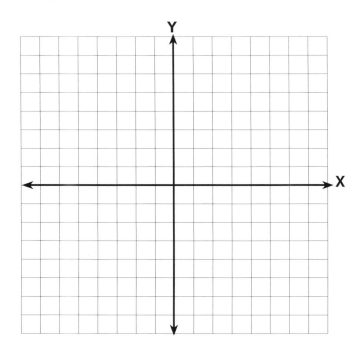

<u>**PART B**</u>

Explain how you graphed each equation and how you knew what the approximate answer was.

       LumosLearning.com

10. **PART A**

Which of the following statements is not a way to calculate the slope of a line that passes through the origin?

Ⓐ $m = \dfrac{y_2 - y_1}{x_2 - x_1}$

Ⓑ If (x_1, y_1) is $(0, 0)$, then $m = \dfrac{y - 0}{x - 0}$

Ⓒ $m = \dfrac{y}{x}$

Ⓓ $m = \dfrac{x_2 - x_1}{y_2 - y_1}$

Ⓔ $y = mx$

PART B

Which of the following statements does not apply to a line that intercepts the y-axis at b?

Ⓐ $m = \dfrac{y_2 - y_2}{x_2 - x_1}$

Ⓑ $m = \dfrac{y - b}{x - 0}$

Ⓒ $m = \dfrac{x - 0}{y - b}$

Ⓓ $mx = y - b$

Ⓔ $y = mx + b$

11. Solve the following equation: $5x + 19 = 314$

   Ⓐ 55
   Ⓑ 57
   Ⓒ 59
   Ⓓ 61
   Ⓔ 63

12. Emily is working on a volume problem. She has a sphere that has a radius of 6 ft. and a cone that also has a radius of 6 ft. and a height that's twice the length of the radius.

   PART A

   What is the volume of the sphere and cone in terms of π?

   PART B

   What is the relationship that exists between the volume of the sphere and the cone?

   Ⓐ The sphere is 4 times the volume of the cone
   Ⓑ The cone is 1/3 the volume of the sphere
   Ⓒ The sphere is 1/3 the volume of the cone
   Ⓓ The cone is 1/2 of the sphere
   Ⓔ There is no relationship between the two volumes.

13. Eugene is washing cars during the summer weekends to help save for a down payment for a car. He washed 7 cars and washed and detailed 10 cars last week. This week, he washed 3 cars and washed and detailed 5 cars. If he earned $1100 last week and $525 this week, how much is it to get your car washed and to get your car washed and detailed?

   Ⓐ $45 for washing and $35 for washing and detailing
   Ⓑ $50 for washing and $75 for washing and detailing
   Ⓒ $35 for washing and $65 for washing and detailing
   Ⓓ $75 for washing and $50 for washing and detailing
   Ⓔ $65 for washing and $75 for washing and detailing

14. Brian is keeping a budget for his monthly expenses. He spends 35% on his mortgage, 17% on his car payment, 13% on utilities, 17% on gas, 5% on food, and the rest on miscellaneous expenses. If he earns $1350 a month, how much money does he left for miscellaneous expenses?

15. Elvis is preparing an area in his yard for a flower garden. He wants to make it three times as long as it is wide. He has 200 feet of decorative stone to surround his flower garden. Write and solve a system of equations to determine the dimensions of his flower garden. Don't forget to define your variables.

   Ⓐ l = 15 ft., w = 25 ft.
   Ⓑ l = 25 ft., w = 75 ft.
   Ⓒ l = 25 ft., w = 15 ft.
   Ⓓ l = 75 ft., w = 25 ft.
   Ⓔ l = 75 ft., w = 15 ft.

16. Which sentence best describes the data in the table below?

x	-2	-1	0	1	2
y	18	15	12	9	6

   Ⓐ Positive linear relationship
   Ⓑ Positive nonlinear relationship
   Ⓒ Negative linear relationship
   Ⓓ Negative nonlinear relationship
   Ⓔ There is no relationship

17. Juan Valdez orders coffee for his restaurant in cylindrical barrels. These barrels are 30 inches tall and have a diameter of 54 inches. What is the volume of the coffee barrels in ft³?

18. Eric's class is running laps around the gym as punishment. After the first few laps, Eric decided that he wasn't going to run the entire way around the gym. He cut across the gym diagonally.

PART A

If the dimensions of the gym were 24 ft. by 45 ft., how much distance did he save on one lap?

PART B

About how many times will he have to take his shortcut to save approximately one full lap?

End of Performance Based Assessment (PBA) - 1

LumosLearning.com   ▲

Performance Based Assessment (PBA) - 1

Answer Key

Question No.	Answer	Related Lumos Online Workbook	CCSS
1 PART A	Yes	Verifying the Pythagorean theorem	8.G.6
1 PART B	*	Verifying the Pythagorean theorem	8.G.6
1 PART C	EG = 15	Verifying the Pythagorean theorem	8.G.6
2	8 dimes and 7 nickels	Solving Systems of equations	8.G.9
3 Part A	*	Compare Proportions	8.EE.5
3 Part B	*	Compare Proportions	8.EE.5
3 Part C	Bus	Compare Proportions	8.EE.5
3 Part D	About 45 minutes before the car	Compare Proportions	8.EE.5
4 PART A	11.25∏ ft³	Finding Volume: Cone, Cylinder and Sphere	8.G.1; 8.G.9
4 PART B	3.75 ∏ ft³	Finding Volume: Cone, Cylinder and Sphere	8.G.1; 8.G.9
5	C	Verifying the Pythagorean theorem	8.G.6
6 PART A	D	Compare Proportions	8.EE.5
6 PART B	C	Compare Proportions	8.EE.5
7 PART A	*	Linear Function Models	8.F.4
7 PART B	*	Linear Function Models	8.F.4
7 PART C	*	Linear Function Models	8.F.4
8	*	Solving Systems of Equations	8.G.9
9 PART A	*	Solving Systems of Equations	8.G.9
9 PART B	*	Solving Systems of Equations	8.G.9
10 PART A	D	Pythagorean Theorem and Coordinate System	8.EE.6
10 PART B	C	Understanding Slope	8.EE.6

* See detailed explanation

Question No.	Answer	Related Lumos Online Workbook	CCSS
11	C	Solving Linear Equations	8.EE.7B
12 PART A	Sphere = 864/3∏ ft³ Cone = 216/3∏ ft³	Finding Volume: Cone, Cylinder and Sphere	8.G.1; 8.G.9
12 PART B	A	Finding Volume: Cone, Cylinder and Sphere	8.G.1; 8.G.9
13	B	Solving Systems of Equations	8.G.9
14	$175.50	Rational vs. Irrational Numbers	8.NS.1
15	D	Solving Systems of Equations	8.G.9
16	C	Analyzing Functions	8.F.5
17	*	Finding Volume: Cone, Cylinder and Sphere	8.G.1; 8.G.9
18 PART A	19 ft	Pythagorean Theorem & Coordinate System	8.G.8
18 PART B	About 8 times	Pythagorean Theorem & Coordinate System	8.G.8

* See detailed explanation

LumosLearning.com   ▲

Performance Based Assessment (PBA) - 1

Detailed Explanations

Question No.	Answer	Detailed Explanation
1 PART A	Yes	Using the Pythagorean theorem, $a^2 + b^2 = c^2$, we substitute 7 for a, 24 for b, and 25 for c. Since it makes a true statement the triangle is a right triangle.
1 PART B		Using the Pythagorean theorem, $a^2 + b^2 = c^2$, we substitute 7 for a, 24 for b, and 25 for c. Since it makes a true statement the triangle is a right triangle.
1 PART C	EG = 15	Use the Pythagorean theorem. If a is 8 and c is 17, we are solving for b. $17^2 - 8^2 = b^2$.
2	8 dimes and 7 nickels	d = dimes, n = nickels d + n = 15 .10d + .05n = 1.15 Multiply the bottom equation by 100 to get rid of the decimals. 10d + 5n = 115. Solve the top equation for n. n = 15-d. Now we can substitute that in the first equation. 10d + 5(15 − d) = 115. Distributing the 5 we get 10d + 75 − 5d = 115. Combining our like terms gives us 5d + 75 = 115. Subtract 75 from both sides leaves us 5d = 40. Dividing gives us d = 8. Substituting that back into the second equation we have n = 15-8, and n = 7.

Question No.	Answer	Detailed Explanation
3 PART A		The car is traveling 15 mph faster than the bus.

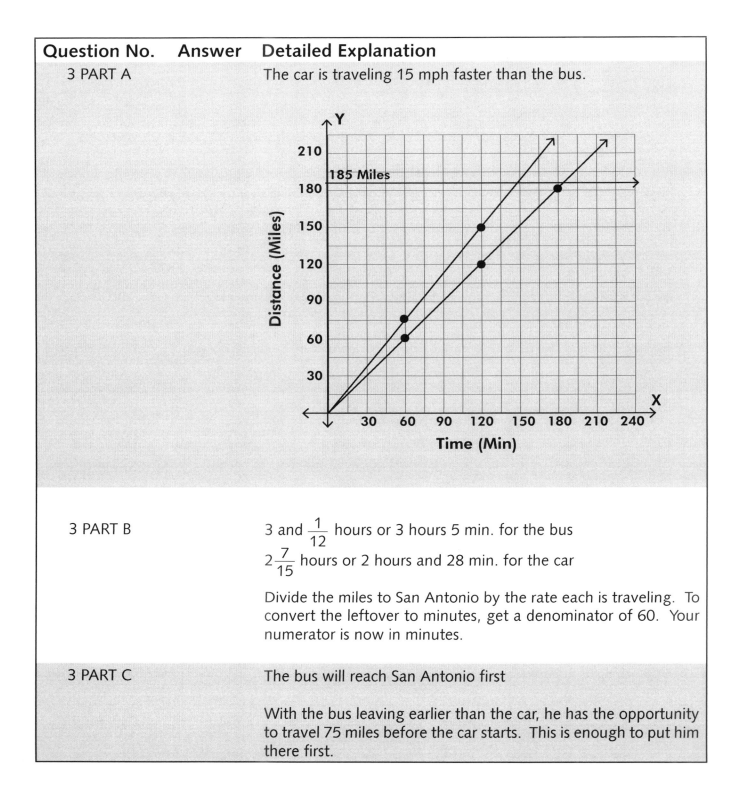

3 PART B

3 and $\frac{1}{12}$ hours or 3 hours 5 min. for the bus

$2\frac{7}{15}$ hours or 2 hours and 28 min. for the car

Divide the miles to San Antonio by the rate each is traveling. To convert the leftover to minutes, get a denominator of 60. Your numerator is now in minutes.

3 PART C

The bus will reach San Antonio first

With the bus leaving earlier than the car, he has the opportunity to travel 75 miles before the car starts. This is enough to put him there first.

    LumosLearning.com   ▲

Question No.	Answer	Detailed Explanation
3 PART D		The bus will reach San Antonio about 45 minutes before the car
		In 1 ¼ hours, the bus has traveled 75 miles and the car is still in Houston. After another hour, the bus has traveled 135 miles and the car is 75 miles out of Houston. At 3 hours, the bus is at 180 miles and the car is at 131.25 miles. Another 5 miles and the bus is in San Antonio. The car still needs to drive about 55 miles to get there, which is about 45 minutes in car time.
4 PART A	11.25∏ in³	Since the diameter is 3 in, that makes the radius 1.5 inches. Square that, gives us 2.25 in². Multiply that by the height of 5 and we get 11.25∏ in³.
4 PART B	3.75∏ in³	Since the formulas are the same with the exception of dividing everything by 3, the only thing we need to do is divide the cylinder volume by 3.
4 PART C	3	The big idea here is that it takes 3 full cones to equal the volume of a cylinder with the same dimensions.
5	C	If $a^2 + b^2 = c^2$, the triangle is a right triangle.
6 PART A	D	Slope is the rise over run. Because the line is falling to the right, that makes it a negative slope. We count down 4 and right 3.
6 PART B	C	Slope is rise over run. Because the line is falling to the right, that makes it a negative slope. We count down 8 and right 6, which gives us -8/6. This simplifies down to -4/3.
6 PART C	B	In making a statement about the triangles, we are looking at the fact that all our sides are proportional. This means we have a similar pair of triangles. Other than making sure we have the symbol for similar, we need to choose the answer that has both triangle written in the same order and corresponding sides are matching up.

7 PART A

S	0	1	2	3	4	5
S²	0	1	4	9	16	25

S	0	1	2	3	4	5
4S	0	4	8	12	16	20

Simply set up the tables and fill in the information based on the rules for each table.

Question No.	Answer	Detailed Explanation
7 PART B		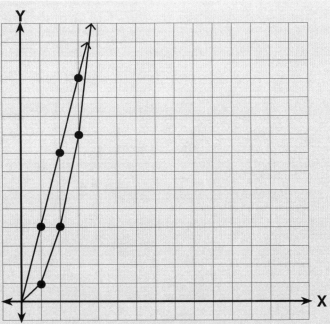
7 PART C		The graph of s^2 is curved while the graph of $4s$ is linear. They are both functions however.
8	Shirts are $15.75 Pants are $21.65	X = cost of shirt, y = cost of pants. $3x + 4y = \$133.85$ $4x + 3y = \$127.95$ Multiply the top equation by -3 and the bottom equation by 4 so the y coefficients will be 12 and -12 and cancel each other out. This leaves us with $7x = \$110.25$. Solve for x and you get $15.75. Take that value and put it back in for x and solve for y. $3(\$15.75) + 4y = \$133.85$. Distributing the 3, we get $47.25 $+ 4y = \$133.85$. Subtract to isolate y and you get $4y = \$86.60$ divide by 4 and a pair of pants cost $21.65.

LumosLearning.com   ▲

Question No.	Answer	Detailed Explanation
9 PART A		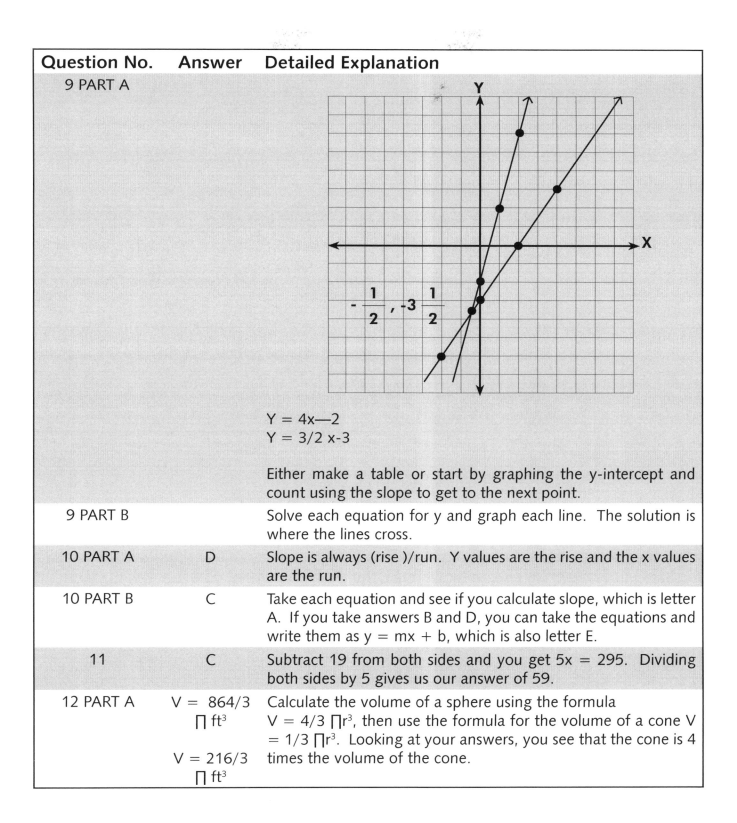 $Y = 4x - 2$ $Y = 3/2 \ x - 3$ Either make a table or start by graphing the y-intercept and count using the slope to get to the next point.
9 PART B		Solve each equation for y and graph each line. The solution is where the lines cross.
10 PART A	D	Slope is always (rise)/run. Y values are the rise and the x values are the run.
10 PART B	C	Take each equation and see if you calculate slope, which is letter A. If you take answers B and D, you can take the equations and write them as $y = mx + b$, which is also letter E.
11	C	Subtract 19 from both sides and you get $5x = 295$. Dividing both sides by 5 gives us our answer of 59.
12 PART A	$V = 864/3$ Π ft³ $V = 216/3$ Π ft³	Calculate the volume of a sphere using the formula $V = 4/3 \ \Pi r^3$, then use the formula for the volume of a cone $V = 1/3 \ \Pi r^3$. Looking at your answers, you see that the cone is 4 times the volume of the cone.

Question No.	Answer	Detailed Explanation
12 PART B	A	Same as PART A
13	$50 for wash $75 for wash and detail	X = car wash, y = car wash and detail. 7x + 10y = 1100 3x + 5y = 525. Multiply the second equation by -2 so the y coefficients are the opposite of each other. X = 50. Substitute back in 3(50) + 5y = 525. 150 + 5y = 525. Subtract 150 from both sides leaves us with 5y = 375. Y has a value of $75.
14	$175.50	Add up the given percents and subtract from 100. That leaves 13% for miscellaneous. If you take the 13%, turn it into a decimal and multiply it by $1350, you get $175.50 for the category.
15	D	2l + 2w = 200, l = 3w. Substitute it in, 2(3w) +2w = 200. 8w = 200. W = 25 ft. L= 3(25) = 75 ft.
16	C	X values are increasing while the y values are decreasing. This will give us a negative y value over a positive x value. It will make a negative slope that is linear.
17	V = 12.7 ft^3	Convert all the inches into feet. You have a height of 2.5 ft. and a radius of 2.25 ft. Now calculate the volume by using V = Bh. Round it to the nearest 10th.
18 PART A	19 ft.	One trip around the gym would be 138 ft. If we cut the diagonal, we use the Pythagorean theorem to find the distance of the hypotenuse, which is 51 ft. One trip with the shortcut is 119 ft. Subtract the 2 and you have 19ft. shorter route than walking the entire perimeter.
18 PART B	8 laps	With a perimeter of 138 ft. and saving 19 ft. with the shortcut, we divide the 2 numbers. 138 divided by 19 gives us 7 trips with some left over. With the left over amount, we can bump it up to 8 laps.

Notes

Performance Based Assessment (PBA) - 2

Student Name: **Start Time:**
Test Date: **End Time:**

> Here are some reminders for when you are taking the Grade 8 Mathematics Performance Based Assessment (PBA).
>
> To answer the questions on the test, use the directions given in the question. If you do not know the answer to a question, skip it and go on to the next question. If time permits, you may return to questions in this session only. Do your best to answer every question.

1. In questions 1 Part A-D, you are given a number. Identify which group(s) each number belongs in. Below each section, explain how you know which group to put each number in.

   PART A

   0

   PART B

   $-3\dfrac{1}{3}$

PART C

π

```



```

PART D

$\sqrt{81}$

```



```

2. What is the difference between a rational number and an irrational number? Give an example of each type of number in your explanation in the box below.

```



```

3. ## PART A

Put the following numbers in order from greatest to least:
$\{9.2314 \times 10^{-4}, 6.71 \times 10^{7}, 7.5 \times 10^{-3}, 6.75 \times 10^{7}, 3.4 \times 10^{8}\}$.

```



```

PART B

How did you determine the order? Write your answer in complete sentence(s).

```
[                                                                    ]
[                                                                    ]
[                                                                    ]
[                                                                    ]
```

4.   Can $0.08\overline{3}$ be written as a fraction?

PART A

If it can, show your work below on how to write it as a fraction.

```
[                                                                    ]
[                                                                    ]
[                                                                    ]
[                                                                    ]
```

PART B

Is this a rational or irrational number?   How do you know?

```
[                                                                    ]
[                                                                    ]
[                                                                    ]
[                                                                    ]
```

5.

PART A

Which of the following numbers could be Point "a" on the number line above?

Ⓐ √2
Ⓑ √(-2)
Ⓒ -√(-2)
Ⓓ -√2
Ⓔ None of the above

PART B

In the box below, explain how you got your answer.

PART C

Which of the following numbers could be point "b" on the number line above?

Ⓐ √2
Ⓑ √(-2)
Ⓒ -√(-2)
Ⓓ -√2
Ⓔ None of the above

PART D

In the box below, explain how you arrived at your answer.

6. Where would you place -2π on the number line below?

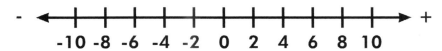

7. There are 13 animals in the barn. Some are chickens and some are pigs. There are 40 legs in all. How many of each animal are there?

PART A

Write a system of equations that you could use to solve this problem in the box below.

PART B

Solve the system you wrote above in the box below.

PART C

Check your answers to make sure you are correct. Explain how you are checking them to justify your solution to the system.

8. The sum of the digits of a certain two-digit number is 7. Reversing its digits increases the number by 9. What is the number?

9. John and Gina are ordering the following set of real numbers from least to greatest: $\{-7, \frac{3}{2}, \sqrt{9}, \pi, -\frac{1}{2}\}$. John said that they should go in the following order $\{, -\frac{1}{2}, -7, \pi, \sqrt{9}, \frac{3}{2}\}$. Gina says they should be in the following order: $\{-7, -\frac{1}{2}, \frac{3}{2}, \sqrt{9}, \pi\}$.

   Who is correct and why? Write your answer in complete sentence(s) below.

10. The distance from the earth to the moon is 238,000 miles.

   PART A

   What is this distance written in scientific notation?

   PART B

   The distance from the earth to the sun is 92,960,000 miles. What is this distance written in scientific notation?

PART C

About how many times further away from the earth is the sun compared to the moon?

PART D

Explain how you arrived at your answer in Part C.

11. The diameter of the earth is about 8,000 miles.

    ### PART A

    Assuming that the earth is a sphere, what is the volume of the earth in mi³ in terms of π?

PART B

The radius of the moon is about 1100 miles. Assuming that the moon is a sphere, what is the volume of the moon in mi³ in terms of π?

```




```

PART C

About how many times greater is the volume of the earth compared to the moon? Show all your work in the box below.

```




```

On questions 12-15, simplify each of the exponent problems. Remember that answers may only contain positive exponents.

12. $(x^{-2} y^{-2})^4$

```




```

13. $(2x^2)^{-4}$

14. $(x^2)^0$

15. $\dfrac{2x^4\ y^{-4}\ z^{-3}}{3x^2\ y^{-3}\ z^4}$

16. If $x^2 = 16$, what is the value of x?

17.   If $y^3 = -125$, what is the value of y?

18.   A boat traveled 336 miles downstream and back. The trip downstream took 12 hours. The trip back took 14 hours.

PART A

What is the speed of the boat in still water?

PART B

What is the speed of the current?

End of Performance Based Assessment (PBA) - 2

Performance Based Assessment (PBA) - 2

Answer Key

Question No.	Answer	Related Lumos Online Workbook	CCSS
1 PART A	Whole, integers, rational, real	Rational Vs. Irrational Numbers	8.NS.1
1 PART B	Rational, real	Rational Vs. Irrational Numbers	8.NS.1
1 PART C	Irrational, real	Rational Vs. Irrational Numbers	8.NS.1
1 PART D	Natural, whole, integer, rational, real	Rational Vs. Irrational Numbers	8.NS.1
2	*	Rational Vs. Irrational Numbers	8.NS.1
3 PART A	*	Scientific Notation	8.EE.3
3 PART B	*	Scientific Notation	8.EE.3
4 PART A	Yes, 1/12	Rational Vs. Irrational Numbers	8.NS.1
4 PART B	*	Rational Vs. Irrational Numbers	8.NS.1
5 PART A	D	Approximating Irrational Numbers	8.NS.2
5 PART B	*	Approximating Irrational Numbers	8.NS.2
5 PART C	A	Approximating Irrational Numbers	8.NS.2
5 PART D	*	Approximating Irrational Numbers	8.NS.2
6	Between -6 and -8.	Approximating Irrational Numbers	8.NS.2
7 PART A	$c + p = 13, 2c + 4p = 40$	Solving Systems of Equations	8.EE.8C
7 PART B	$c = 6, p = 7$	Solving Systems of Equations	8.EE.8C
7 PART C	*	Solving Systems of Equations	8.EE.8C
8	Original number = 34	Solving Systems of Equations	8.EE.8C
9	Gina	Rational vs. Irrational Numbers	8.NS.1
10 PART A	2.38×10^5 miles	Scientific Notation	8.EE.3
10 PART B	9.296×10^7 miles	Scientific Notation	8.EE.3

* See detailed explanation

Question No.	Answer	Related Lumos Online Workbook	CCSS
10 PART C	About 400 times	Solving Problems Involving Scientific Notation	8.EE.4
10 PART D	*	Solving Problems Involving Scientific Notation	8.EE.4
11 PART A	$v = \dfrac{2.048 \times 10^{12}}{3}$	Solving Problems Involving Scientific Notation Finding Volume: Cone, Cylinder, Sphere	8.EE.4; 8.G.9
11 PART B	$v = \dfrac{1.331 \times 10^{9}}{3}$	Solving Problems Involving Scientific Notation Finding Volume: Cone, Cylinder, Sphere	8.EE.4; 8.G.9
11 PART C	Approximately 2000 times	Solving Problems Involving Scientific Notation	8.EE.4
12	$\dfrac{1}{x^8 y^8}$	Properties of Exponents	8.EE.1
13	$\dfrac{1}{16x^8}$	Properties of Exponents	8.EE.1
14	1	Properties of Exponents	8.EE.1
15	$\dfrac{2x^2}{3yz^7}$	Properties of Exponents	8.EE.1
16	$x = \pm 4$	Square and Cube Roots	8.EE.2
17	$y = -5$	Square and Cube Roots	8.EE.2
18 PART A	26 miles per hour	Solving Systems of Equations	8.EE.8C
18 PART B	2 miles per hour	Solving Systems of Equations	8.EE.8C

* **See detailed explanation**

LumosLearning.com ▼

Performance Based Assessment (PBA) - 2

Detailed Explanations

Question No.	Answer	Detailed Explanation
1 PART A	Whole, integers, rational, real	Zero starts the whole number group. As the groups work their way out, the numbers from the inner-most groups become part of the outer groups.
1 PART B	Rational, real	Fractions and repeating decimals are part of Rational Numbers and they are Real numbers.
1 Part C	Irrational, real	Decimals that don't repeat or terminate are always irrational numbers and real numbers.
1 Part D	Natural, whole, integer, rational, real	Natural numbers are numbers found in nature. They don't include 0, but do include the counting numbers. Because this is the inner most group, it is part of every outer group.
2		Rational numbers can be written as fractions, both proper and improper, and include decimals that terminate or repeat, as they can also be written as fractions. Ex: $\sqrt{4}$, 1/3, -1/4. Irrational numbers are decimals that can't be written as fractions and don't repeat or terminate. Ex: π, $\sqrt{2}$, 0.010110111...
3 PART A		3.4×10^8, 6.75×10^7, 6.71×10^7, 7.5×10^{-3}, 9.234×10^{-4}
3 PART B		The greater the exponent, the greater the value of the number. You are moving the decimal point more places. When the exponent is the same, put the numbers in order by the base number.
4 PART A	Yes, 1/12	If $x = 0.8\overline{3}$, then $1000x = 83.\overline{3}$ and $100x = 8.\overline{3}$ $1000x = 83.\overline{3}$ $-100x = 8.\overline{3}$ $\overline{900x = 75}$ $\dfrac{900x = 75}{900 \qquad 900}$ $x = 1/12$

Question No.	Answer	Detailed Explanation
4 PART B		It is rational because it is a repeating decimal that we can write as a fraction.
5 PART A	D	
5 PART B		"a" is between-1 and -2. Our answer also needs to be between that. -1 can also be written as -√1 and -2 can be written as -√4. -√2 falls right between the two perfect square roots.
5 PART C	A	
5 PART D		"b" is between 1 and 2. Our answer also needs to be between that. 1 can also be written as √1 and 2 can be written as √4. √2 falls right between the two perfect square roots.
6	Between -6 and -8.	-2π is approximately -6.28. This will fall between -6 and -10.
7 PART A	c + p = 13,2c + 4p = 40	c = chickens, p = pigs. Each chicken has 2 legs and each pig has 4 legs. c+p=13 2c+4p=40
7 PART B	c = 6, p = 7	Multiply the first equation by -2 to get the opposite coefficient in front of c and you get -2c+(-2p)=-26 2c+4p=40 Chickens cancel out and you are left with 2p=14 Divide both sides by 2 and p=7. c+p=13 c+7=13 Subtract 7 from both sides and c=6.
7 PART C		6+7=13 13=13 2(6)+4(7)=40 12+28=40 40=40 By substituting the values back into both equations for c and p, we see that both equations give us matching answers. This means we have found the solution for this system of equations.

 LumosLearning.com ▼

Question No.	Answer	Detailed Explanation
8	Original number = 34	x = first digit, y = second digit Adding the digits together does not include place value for the first equation. $$x+y=7$$ In the second equation, place value matters. Reversing the digits means y is in the 10s column and x is in the ones. Using this information, we get the following equation: $$10y+x=(10x+y)+9$$ By combining like terms and solving for x, we get: $$x=10x-9y+9$$ $$-9x=-9y+9$$ $$\frac{-9x=-9y+9}{-9}$$ $$x=y-1$$ We take this answer and substitute it back into the first equation for x and solve for y. $$(y-1)+y=7$$ $$2y=8$$ $$y=4$$ Now we can use this value to get our value of x. $$x+4=7$$ $$x=3$$ Our original number was xy, so by substituting the numbers in for the variables, we get our answer of 34 for the original number.
9	Gina	Gina's numbers start off with -7. John's numbers start off with -1/2. Because -7 is further away from 0, it is the smaller value. Therefore, Gina is correct.
10 PART A	2.38×10^5 miles	Simply move the decimal point until you get a number between 1 and 10. Your exponent will always be the number of times you moved the decimal point. It's a positive decimal because the original number is greater than 1.
10 PART B	9.296×10^7 miles	Simply move the decimal point until you get a number between 1 and 10. Your exponent will always be the number of times you moved the decimal point. It's a positive decimal because the original number is greater than 1.
10 PART C	About 400 times	

Question No.	Answer	Detailed Explanation
10 PART D		Divide both numbers while written in scientific notation. $$\frac{9.296 \times 10^7}{2.38 \times 10^5}$$ Divide the whole numbers and you get about 4. Divide (subtract) the exponents and you get 10^2. $$4 \times 100 = 400$$
11 PART A	$v = \dfrac{2.048 \times 10^{12}}{3}$	$V = \dfrac{4}{3}\pi r^3$ $V = \dfrac{4}{3}\pi(8 \times 10^3)^3$ $V = \dfrac{4}{3}\pi 512 \times 10^9$ $V = \dfrac{2.048 \times 10^9}{3}\pi \text{ mi}^3$ $V = \dfrac{2.048 \times 10^{12}}{3}\pi \text{ mi}^3$
11 PART B	$v = \dfrac{1.331 \times 10^9}{3}$	$V = \dfrac{1.331 \times 10^9}{3}\pi \text{ mi}^3$
11 PART C	Approximately 2000 times	$\dfrac{2.048 \times 10^{12}}{3}\pi \text{ mi}^3$ $\div \dfrac{1.331 \times 10^9}{3}\pi \text{ mi}^3$ $\dfrac{2.048 \times 10^{12}\pi}{3} \times \dfrac{3}{1.331 \times 10^9 \pi}$ $\dfrac{2.048 \times 10^{12}}{1.331 \times 10^9}$ about 2×10^3 or 2000 times
12	$\dfrac{1}{x^8 y^8}$	$(x^{-2}y^{-2})^4$ $x^{-8}y^{-8}$: Distribute the 4 to both exponents $\dfrac{1}{x^8 y^8}$ In order to make negative exponents positive, we write the reciprocal of the original number. Since both x and y appear in the numerator, they will be in the opposite place (denominator) in our answer.

 LumosLearning.com ▼

Question No.	Answer	Detailed Explanation
13	$\dfrac{1}{16x^8}$	$(2x^2)^{-4}$ $\dfrac{1}{(2x^2)^4}$: Again, to turn the exponent positive, write the original expression as its reciprocal. $\dfrac{1}{16x^8}$: Distribute the 4 to the 2 and the exponent on the variable.
14	1	Anything to the power of zero is 1.
15	$\dfrac{2x^2}{3yz^7}$	$\dfrac{2}{3} \times \dfrac{x^4}{x^2} \times \dfrac{y^{-4}}{y^{-3}} \times \dfrac{z^{-3}}{z^4}$: Look at each part separately. $$\dfrac{2}{3}$$ $$\dfrac{x^4}{x^2} = x^2$$ $$\dfrac{y^{-4}}{y^{-3}} = \dfrac{y^3}{y^4} = \dfrac{1}{y}$$ $$\dfrac{z^{-3}}{z^4} = \dfrac{1}{z^{4+3}} = \dfrac{1}{z^7}$$ Put everything back together: $$\dfrac{2}{3} \times x^2 \times \dfrac{1}{y} \times \dfrac{1}{z^7} = \dfrac{2x^2}{3yz^7}$$
16	$x = \pm 4$	When you introduce the square root in a problem, you have to write both the positive and negative answer.
17	$y = -5$	When finding the cube root, you must think to yourself, "what number times itself 3 times is going to give me the number, in this case – 125, that I'm looking for? Because you are multiplying the same number 3 times, it has to be negative to get a negative answer. 5 raised to the power of 3 gives you 125. Put them together and you get an answer of -5.

Question No.	Answer	Detailed Explanation
18 PART A	26 miles per hour	$d=rt$ $r+c=$going against the current $r-c=$going with the current $336=(r-c)12$ It will take less time going with the current because you will be traveling faster, as the current will be pushing you along. $336=(r+c)14$ It will take more time going back because the current is pushing against you. This will cause you to move at a slower rate. Solve both equations for rate and current and you get: $336/12 \ r-c$ $24=r-c$ $336/14=r+c$ $28=r+c$ Adding both equations to solve for the rate gives us: $28=r+c$ $\underline{24=r-c}$ $52=2r$ $(52=2r)/2$ $r=26$ The speed of the boat in still water is 26 mph.
18 PART B	2 miles per hour	If the rate is 26, we substitute that back in to determine the speed of the current. $28=r+c$ $28=26+c$ $2=c$ We can also substitute it into the second equation to make sure that the answer is the same. $24=r-c$ $24=26-c$ $-2=-c$ $2=c$ Therefore, the speed of the current is 2 mph.

LumosLearning.com   ▼

Notes

End-Of-Year Assessment (EOY) - 1

Student Name:

Test Date:

Start Time:

End Time:

Here are some reminders for when you are taking the Grade 8 Mathematics End-of-Year Assessment (EOY).

To answer the questions on the test, use the directions given in the question. If you do not know the answer to a question, skip it and go on to the next question. If time permits, you may return to questions in this session only. Do your best to answer every question.

1. **Which of the following is not a rational number?**

    Ⓐ $\frac{1}{2}$

    Ⓑ $\sqrt{4}$

    Ⓒ $0.08\overline{3}$

    Ⓓ $\sqrt{7}$

    Ⓔ $0.\overline{01}$

2. **Between which two numbers will the $\sqrt{30}$ be?**

    Ⓐ 0 and 1
    Ⓑ -2 and -3
    Ⓒ 4 and 5
    Ⓓ -5 and -6
    Ⓔ 5 and 6

3. **4.756×10^7 is equivalent to which number in standard notation?**

    Ⓐ 4.7560000
    Ⓑ .0000004756
    Ⓒ 4.756×10^{-7}
    Ⓓ $\frac{4.756}{7}$
    Ⓔ 47,560,000

     LumosLearning.com ◀

4. Which of the following expressions are equivalent to each other? There may be more than one answer.

Ⓐ $\dfrac{1}{49}$

Ⓑ $\dfrac{1}{7^2}$

Ⓒ $7^4 \times 7^{-6}$

Ⓓ 7^2

Ⓔ 7^{-2}

5. Which of the following ordered pairs represents a function?

Ⓐ $\{(0, 5), (8, 3), (7, 6), (0, 2)\}$
Ⓑ $\{(1, 8), (1, 7), (1, 9), (1, 0)\}$
Ⓒ $\{(-1, 2), (-2, 3), (-4, 9), (-1, 7)\}$
Ⓓ $\{(7, 5), (3, 5), (1, 5), (-3, 5)\}$
Ⓔ $\{(7, 3), (2, 6), (3, 8), (2, 5)\}$

6. **PART A**

Select the correct ending(s) to this sentence: **A set of points is a function if and only if**

Ⓐ each output has exactly one input.
Ⓑ each input has exactly one output.
Ⓒ each y is paired with only one x.
Ⓓ there is no correct answer.
Ⓔ each x is paired with one and only one y.

PART B

Which of the following functions are linear?

Ⓐ $y = x+3$
Ⓑ $y = x^2$
Ⓒ $A = \pi r^2$
Ⓓ $P = 2l+2w$
Ⓔ $y = x$

7. **PART A**

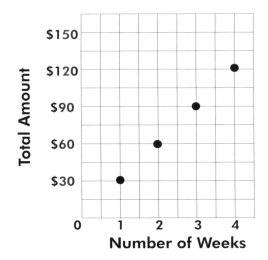

What is the unit rate of the graph above?

A $60 per week
B 1/$30 per week
C $45 per week
D $120 per week
E $30 per week

PART B

What is the unit rate written as a fraction?

A $\dfrac{\$45}{1}$

B $\dfrac{\$60}{1}$

C $\dfrac{\$30}{1}$

D $\dfrac{\$120}{1}$

E $\dfrac{1}{\$30}$

      LumosLearning.com

PART C

If w = the number of weeks and T = total amount, what is the equation that represents the information in the graph?

Ⓐ T=50w
Ⓑ w = 30T
Ⓒ T = 1/30 w
Ⓓ T = $30w
Ⓔ w = $45T

8.   The closest the planet Venus gets to earth is about 25 million miles.

PART A

What is this distance expressed in scientific notation?

Ⓐ 2.5×10^1
Ⓑ 2.5×10^2
Ⓒ 2.5×10^5
Ⓓ 2.5×10^6
Ⓔ 2.5×10^7

PART B

If the space shuttle travels about 17,500 mph in orbit, about how many hours will it take the shuttle to reach Venus?

Ⓐ About 1.43 hours
Ⓑ About 14.3 hours
Ⓒ About 143 hours
Ⓓ About 1, 430 hours
Ⓔ About 14, 300 hours

9.   Given Rectangle ABCD, with point A (1, 5), Point B (7, 5), Point C (7, 2), and Point D (1, 2).

PART A

Find the coordinates of D' after a rotation of 90° counterclockwise around the origin.

Ⓐ (2, 1)
Ⓑ (-1, 2)
Ⓒ (-2, -1)
Ⓓ (2, -1)
Ⓔ (-2, 1)

PART B

If the rectangle is now translated 5 units right and 3 units down, find the coordinates of D''.

Ⓐ (3, -2)
Ⓑ (7, -2)
Ⓒ (-2, 3)
Ⓓ (-3, 2)
Ⓔ (7, -4)

PART C

If the rectangle is now dilated by a scale factor of $\frac{2}{3}$, what would be the coordinates of D'''?

Ⓐ $\left(\frac{14}{3}, \frac{-4}{3} \right)$

Ⓑ $\left(\frac{-4}{3}, 2 \right)$

Ⓒ $\left(\frac{14}{3}, \frac{-8}{3} \right)$

Ⓓ $\left(2, \frac{-4}{3} \right)$

Ⓔ $\left(\frac{-8}{3}, \frac{14}{3} \right)$

PART D

If we now reflect this point over the x-axis, what are the coordinates of D''''?

Ⓐ $\left(\frac{14}{3}, \frac{4}{3} \right)$

Ⓑ $\left(\frac{-4}{3}, -2 \right)$

Ⓒ $\left(\frac{8}{3}, \frac{-14}{3} \right)$

Ⓓ $\left(\frac{-14}{3}, \frac{8}{3} \right)$

Ⓔ $\left(2, \frac{4}{3} \right)$

10. Parallel lines m and n are cut by transversal t forming the 8 angles below.

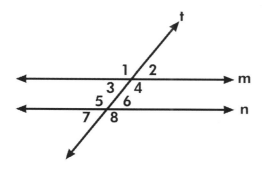

    Ⓐ ∠1 = ∠3
    Ⓑ ∠2 = ∠6
    Ⓒ ∠3 = ∠6
    Ⓓ ∠3 = ∠5
    Ⓔ ∠7 = ∠2

11. Which of the following transformations preserves congruence?

    Ⓐ translation
    Ⓑ dilation
    Ⓒ reflection
    Ⓓ rotation
    Ⓔ none of the above

12. Which of the following can be used to find the lengths of the sides of right ΔABC when 2 of the sides are known?

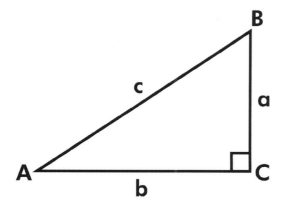

Ⓐ $a^2 + c^2 = b^2$
Ⓑ $a^2 + b^2 = c^2$
Ⓒ $a + b = c$
Ⓓ $(a+b)/2=c$
Ⓔ $b+c=a$

13. **PART A**

In ΔABC below, if $\angle A=45°$ and $\angle B=55°$, what is the measure of $\angle X$?

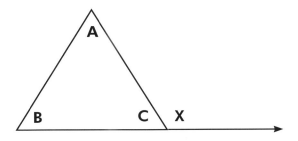

Ⓐ 80°
Ⓑ 45°
Ⓒ 100°
Ⓓ 125°
Ⓔ 110°

PART B

Using the same diagram, if $\angle X=155°$ and $\angle A=35°$, what is the measure of $\angle B$?

Ⓐ 35°
Ⓑ 45°
Ⓒ 95°
Ⓓ 120°
Ⓔ 125°

14. Which of the following is a solution for the equation $x^3=216$

Ⓐ 3
Ⓑ 4
Ⓒ 5
Ⓓ 6
Ⓔ 7

15. Point A (4, -2) and point B (-2, -8) are graphed in the coordinate plane.

PART A

Apply a dilation of -5/2, centered at the origin to both points. What are the coordinates of point B'?

Ⓐ (5, 20)
Ⓑ (-5/8, 5/4)
Ⓒ (10, -5)
Ⓓ (5, -20)
Ⓔ (-5, -20)

PART B

Rotate the line segment 90° clockwise about the origin. What are the coordinates of A''?

Ⓐ (-5, -10)
Ⓑ (10, -5)
Ⓒ (5, -10)
Ⓓ (10, 5)
Ⓔ (5, 10)

PART C

Now reflect this line segment over the y-axis. What are the coordinates of B'''?

Ⓐ (-20, 5)
Ⓑ (-20, -5)
Ⓒ (5, -20)
Ⓓ (-5, 20)
Ⓔ (20, -5)

PART D

Now apply a translation of 5 units right and 5 units down. What are the coordinates of A''''B''''?

Ⓐ A''''(-20, -5), B''''(-5, 10)
Ⓑ A''''(5, 10), B''''(20, -5)
Ⓒ A''''(0, 5), B''''(-15, -10)
Ⓓ A''''(-5, -10), B''''(-20, 5)
Ⓔ A''''(-15, -10), B''''(0, 5)

16.   **PART A**

What is the decimal that represents the fraction 7/8?

Ⓐ 7.8
Ⓑ 8.7
Ⓒ .87
Ⓓ .875
Ⓔ .88

PART B

Which of the following choices best describes the fraction 7/8? There may be more than one correct answer.

Ⓐ Irrational
Ⓑ Mixed number
Ⓒ Proper
Ⓓ Improper
Ⓔ Rational

17.   A farmhouse shelters 23 animals. Some are goats and some are ducks. Altogether there are 58 legs. How many of each animal are there?

Ⓐ 8 ducks, 15 goats
Ⓑ 17 ducks, 6 goats
Ⓒ 16 ducks, 7 goats
Ⓓ 19 ducks, 4 goats
Ⓔ 11 ducks, 12 goats

18.   The exterior angle of a triangle is

Ⓐ equal to 90°.
Ⓑ equal to 180° minus the sum of the 2 non-adjacent angels.
Ⓒ equal to 3 times the sum of the 2 non-adjacent angles.
Ⓓ equal to 180° minus the adjacent angle.
Ⓔ equal to half of 180° minus the adjacent angle.

19. The perimeter of a rectangle is 26 meters. The length of the rectangle is 5 less than twice the width. Find the length and the width of the rectangle.

PART A

Choose which system of equations you'd use to solve this problem.

Ⓐ $2l + 2w = 26, l = 2w - 5$
Ⓑ $l + w = 26, l = 2w - 5$
Ⓒ $2l + 2w = 26, l = 5 - 2w$
Ⓓ $l + w = 13, l = 5 - 2w$
Ⓔ $2l + 2w = 13, l = (w-5)/2$

PART B

Choose the correct solutions to the system of equations.

Ⓐ $w=7, l = 6$
Ⓑ $w=6.5, l = 13$
Ⓒ $w=6, l = 7$
Ⓓ $w=5, l = 8$
Ⓔ $w=4, l = 9$

20. Use the table below to answer the Part A and B.

x	0	1	2	3	4	5
y	4	7	10	13	16	19

PART A

Which equation was used to generate the table?

Ⓐ $y = 4x + 4$
Ⓑ $y = x^2 + 4$
Ⓒ $y = 2x - 4$
Ⓓ $y = x + 4$
Ⓔ $y = 3x + 4$

PART B

What is the rate of change in the above table?

Ⓐ 2
Ⓑ 3
Ⓒ 4
Ⓓ 5
Ⓔ 6

PART C

Use the linear equation from Part A to compare to the table below. Which statement best describes the relationship between the two tables?

x	3	6	9	12	15	18
y	-10	-16	-22	-28	-34	-40

Ⓐ They have the same slope.
Ⓑ The table above has a steeper slope than the table in Part A.
Ⓒ The table above is not a linear function.
Ⓓ The table from Part A has a steeper slope than the table above.
Ⓔ There is no relationship between the two tables.

21. The distance that Eric can travel by driving to work can be represented by a linear equation because he sets his cruise control and is moving at a constant rate. He drives at a rate of 75 mph on the interstate for a total of 1.5 hours.

PART A

What is the linear equation that can be used to find the distance that Eric travels each day?

Ⓐ $d = rt$
Ⓑ $d = t/r$
Ⓒ $d = r/t$
Ⓓ $d = r + t$
Ⓔ $d = 75r$

PART B

What is the total distance that Eric travels each day?

Ⓐ 37.5 miles
Ⓑ 75 miles
Ⓒ 112.5 miles
Ⓓ 150 miles
Ⓔ 187.5 miles

22. **PART A**

Which rational number is equivalent to $0.8\overline{3}$?

Ⓐ $\dfrac{1}{6}$

Ⓑ $\dfrac{1}{3}$

Ⓒ $\dfrac{1}{9}$

Ⓓ $\dfrac{4}{9}$

Ⓔ $\dfrac{5}{6}$

PART B

What is the decimal equivalent of $4\dfrac{5}{6}$?

Ⓐ 4.125
Ⓑ $4.\overline{3}$
Ⓒ 4.5
Ⓓ 4.625
Ⓔ 4.7

23. Consider the equation below and the relationship it represents:

$y = 7x - 9$

PART A

Which of the following statements best describes the relationship?

- Ⓐ Decreasing non-linear function
- Ⓑ Increasing linear function
- Ⓒ Increasing non-linear function
- Ⓓ Decreasing linear function
- Ⓔ There is no relationship

PART B

What would happen to the rate of change if the equation was changed to $y = \dfrac{1}{7} x - 9$?

- Ⓐ The rate of change decreases.
- Ⓑ The rate of change increases.
- Ⓒ There is no change.
- Ⓓ It becomes a non-function.
- Ⓔ None of the above.

24. **PART A**

Which of the following answer choices are not affected by dilating a figure?

- Ⓐ Similarity
- Ⓑ Perimeter
- Ⓒ Angle measures
- Ⓓ Shape of the original figure
- Ⓔ Area

PART B

If ΔABC has points at A(0, 0), B(6, -4), and C(8, 0) and is dilated by a scale factor of -1/2, which statement(s) about ΔABC and ΔA'B'C' is/are true?

Ⓐ m∠B = m∠B'
Ⓑ m∠A = m∠C' A' B'
Ⓒ ΔABC ≅ ΔA'B'C'
Ⓓ m∠C = m∠ AC'B
Ⓔ ΔABC ~ ΔA'B'C'

25. **PART A**

Between which 2 numbers on a number line will √20 be found?

Ⓐ 2 and 3
Ⓑ 3 and 4
Ⓒ 4 and 5
Ⓓ 5 and 6
Ⓔ 6 and 7

PART B

What is a good decimal approximation of √20?

Ⓐ 3.1
Ⓑ 2.2
Ⓒ 5.3
Ⓓ 4.4
Ⓔ 6.5

26. A number whose decimal form never terminates or repeats is called _____?

Ⓐ Simplified
Ⓑ Mixed number
Ⓒ Fraction
Ⓓ Rational
Ⓔ Irrational

27. **Which of the following answers is the simplified form of $3^2 \times 3^{-6}$?**

    Ⓐ 81

    Ⓑ 18

    Ⓒ $\dfrac{1}{81}$

    Ⓓ -18

    Ⓔ $\dfrac{1}{27}$

28. **PART A**

    Which of the following represents a solution to the equation $d^3 = 343$?

    Ⓐ $\sqrt[3]{343}$
    Ⓑ $\sqrt[2]{343}$
    Ⓒ 27
    Ⓓ 18
    Ⓔ $4\sqrt[3]{343}$

    PART B

    Solve the equation from Part A.

    Ⓐ 14
    Ⓑ 7
    Ⓒ 6
    Ⓓ 8
    Ⓔ 18

     LumosLearning.com

For questions 29-31, use the 6 scatterplots below.

Example Scatter Plots

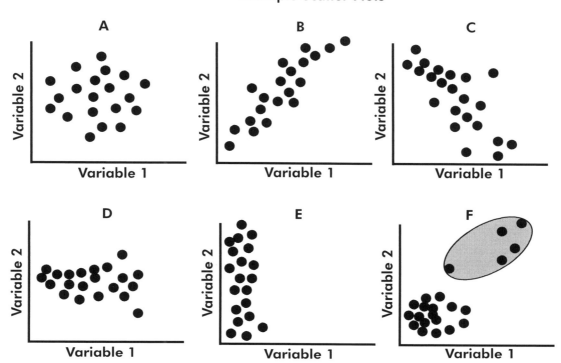

29.   What information can we assume from Scatterplot B? Choose all that apply.

    Ⓐ **Outliers**
    Ⓑ **Negative association**
    Ⓒ **Linear association**
    Ⓓ **No association**
    Ⓔ **Positive association**

30.   What information can we assume from Scatterplot F?

    Ⓐ **Outliers**
    Ⓑ **Negative association**
    Ⓒ **Clustering**
    Ⓓ **No association**
    Ⓔ **Positive association**

31. What information can we assume about Scatterplot C?

(A) Outliers
(B) Negative association
(C) Linear association
(D) Positive association
(E) No association

Use the following question for problems 32 and 33.

If the temperature on a Celsius scale is multiplied by 2 and added to four times the reading on a Fahrenheit scale, the result is 82. Nine times the Celsius reading plus the Fahrenheit reading is -22.

32. The Celsius temperature is:

(A) -1°
(B) -2°
(C) -3°
(D) -4°
(E) -5°

33. The Fahrenheit temperature is:

(A) 23°
(B) 24°
(C) 25°
(D) 26°
(E) 27°

End of End-Of-Year Assessment (EOY) - 1

End-Of-Year Assessment (EOY) -1
Answer Key

Question No.	Answer	Related Lumos Online Workbook	CCSS
1	D	Rational Vs. Irrational Numbers	8.NS.1
2	E	Approximating Rational Numbers	8.NS.2
3	E	Scientific Notation	8.EE.3
4	A, B, C, E	Properties of Exponents	8.EE.1
5	B, C	Analyzing Functions	8.F.5
6 PART A	B, E	Analyzing Functions	8.F.5
6 PART B	A, D, E	Analyzing Functions	8.F.5
7 PART A	E	Understanding Slope	8.EE.6
7 PART B	C	Understanding Slope	8.EE.6
7 PART C	D	Understanding Slope	8.EE.6
8 PART A	E	Scientific Notation	8.EE.3
8 PART B	D	Solving Problems Involving Scientific Notation	8.EE.4
9 PART A	E	Analyzing Transformations	8.G.3
9 PART B	A	Analyzing Transformations	8.G.3
9 PART C	D	Analyzing Transformations	8.G.3
9 PART D	E	Analyzing Transformations	8.G.3
10	B, C, E	Interior & Exterior Angles in Geometric Figures	8.G.5
11	A, C, D	Transformations of Congruency	8.G.2
12	B	Verifying the Pythagorean Theorem	8.G.6
13 PART A	C	Interior & Exterior Angles in Geometric Figures	8.G.5
13 PART B	E	Interior & Exterior Angles in Geometric Figures	8.G.5
14	D	Square and Cube Roots	8.EE.2
15 PART A	A	Analyzing Transformations	8.G.3
15 PART B	E	Analyzing Transformations	8.G.3
15 PART C	B	Analyzing Transformations	8.G.3
15 PART D	C	Analyzing Transformations	8.G.3
16 PART A	D	Rational Vs. Irrational Numbers	8.NS.1
16 PART B	C, E	Rational Vs. Irrational Numbers	8.NS.1

Question No.	Answer	Related Lumos Online Workbook	CCSS
17	B	Solving Systems of Equations	8.EE.8C
18	B, D	Interior & Exterior Angles in Geometric Figures	8.G.5
19 PART A	A	Solving Systems of Equations	8.EE.8C
19 PART B	C	Solving Systems of Equations	8.EE.8C
20 PART A	E	Analyzing Functions	8.F.5
20 PART B	B	Analyzing Functions	8.F.5
20 PART C	D	Comparing Functions	8.F.2
21 PART A	A	Linear Functions	8.F.3
21 PART B	C	Linear Functions	8.F.3
22 PART A	E	Rational Vs. Irrational Numbers	8.NS.1
22 PART B	D	Rational Vs. Irrational Numbers	8.NS.1
23 PART A	B	Linear Functions	8.F.3
23 PART B	A	Linear Functions	8.F.3
24 PART A	A, B, C, D	Transformations and Similarity	8.G.4
24 PART B	A, B, E	Transformations and Similarity	8.G.4
25 PART A	C	Approximating Irrational Numbers	8.NS.2
25 PART B	D	Approximating Irrational Numbers	8.NS.2
26	E	Rational Vs. Irrational Numbers	8.NS.1
27	C	Properties of Exponents	8.EE.1
28 PART A	A	Square and Cube Roots	8.EE.2
28 PART B	B	Square and Cube Roots	8.EE.2
29	C, E	Analyzing Linear Scatter Plots	8.SP.3
30	A, C, D	Analyzing Linear Scatter Plots	8.SP.3
31	B, C	Analyzing Linear Scatter Plots	8.SP.3
32	E	Solving Systems of Equations	8.EE.8C
33	A	Solving Systems of Equations	8.EE.8C

End-Of-Year Assessment (EOY) -1

Detailed Explanations

Question No.	Answer	Detailed Explanation
1	D	Rational numbers can be written as fractions and include decimals that repeat or terminate. Every answer meets these qualifications except √7.
2	E	$5^2 = 25$ and $6^2 = 36$. √30 falls between these two numbers.
3	E	Move the decimal point 7 places to the right.
4	A, B, C, E	All of the answers are equivalent to 7^{-2} which is $1/7^2$ because exponents must always be written as positive, not negative numbers.
5	B, C	A function cannot have x-values that repeat.
6 PART A	B, E	Input and x are the same, as output and y. A function can only have one x for each y. Both B and E state this using different vocabulary.
6 PART B	A, D, E	Linear functions cannot have exponents at all.
7 PART A	E	Unit rate is how much for one. In this graph, the rate is $30 a week.
7 PART B	C	To write the unit rate as a fraction, we simply put the whole number over 1.
7 PART C	D	The total amount is equation to $30 times the number of weeks. Letter D translates this equation properly.
8 PART A	E	First, you need to write 25 million as 25,000,000. Then you can put it into scientific notation.
8 PART B	D	Turn 17, 500 into scientific notation and divide. You get about 1.43×10^3, which is the same as letter D.
9 PART A	E	A counterclockwise rotation results in taking the original coordinates and switching places, making the original y-value negative. Instead of (x, y) you end up with (-y, x).
9 PART B	A	Moving right 5 and up 3, you get (3, -2).
9 PART C	D	Multiply the above coordinates by 2/3, and you have (2, -4/3).
9 PART D	E	When you reflect over the x-axis the y-value changes. Instead of negative, we now have a positive 4/3.
10	B, C, E	B is corresponding angles, C is Alternate Interior Angles, and E is Alternate Exterior Angles.

Question No.	Answer	Detailed Explanation
11	A, C, D	Preserving congruence is translation, reflection, and rotation. They don't change the size, just the location of a shape on the coordinate plane
12	B	The Pythagorean theorem works only on right triangles and states that $a^2 + b^2 = c^2$.
13 PART A	C	In order to get the exterior angle, one must add together the two non-adjacent angles, angle A and B in this triangle.
13 PART B	E	To find one of the non-adjacent interior angles, we do the opposite which is take the exterior and subtract the non-adjacent angle we are given.
14	D	Figure out what number you must multiply by itself 3 times to get a total of 216. Only 6 will work.
15 PART A	A	Multiply both points by the scale factor to get the new points.
15 PART B	E	In order to get this answer, we must first apply the scale factor then change the coordinates. To graph a clockwise rotation, you switch x and y, and make the original x-value negative (y, -x)
15 PART C	B	Once again, take the original B and apply the transformations from Part A and B, then to reflect it over the y-axis, the x-value becomes the opposite.
15 PART D	C	Apply the first 3 transformations to both points, then move each point right 5 and down 5.
16 PART A	D	Divide 8 into 7.
16 PART B	C, E	The fraction is proper and rational.
17	B	Let d = # of ducks and g = # of goats $d+g=23$ $2d+4g=58$ Multiply the first equation by -2 to cancel the variable d. $-2d-2g=-46$ $2d+4g=58$ Add them together and you get $2g=12$ Divide both sides by 2 and $g=6$ Substitute that back in to the first equation $d+6=13$ Subtract 6 from both sides and $d=17$

LumosLearning.com ◄

Question No.	Answer	Detailed Explanation
18	B, D	The exterior angle is supplementary to the adjacent angle and the same as the sum of the two non-adjacent angles.
19 PART A	A	Letter A is the only choice that has the correct perimeter formula for a rectangle and the correct formula for the length.
19 PART B	C	Work out the solution by substituting the second equation back in to the first for the length. $$2(2w-5)+2w=26$$ $$4w-10+2w=26$$ $$6w-10=26$$ $$6w=36$$ $$w=6$$ Substitute w back in to the equation to find the length. $$l=2(6)-5$$ $$l=12-5$$ $$l=7$$
20 PART A	E	Try each x-value into each equation until you find the right one that works.
20 PART B	B	Look at (change in y)/(change in x). This gives you the rate of change.
20 PART C	D	Compare the rate of change in the first table with the rate of change in the second table.
21 PART A	A	$d=rt$
21 PART B	C	To calculate the distance, take the rate of 75 mph times the time, which is 1.5 hours.
22 PART A	E	$$let\ x=0.8\overline{3}$$ $$100x=83.\overline{3}$$ $$10x=8.\overline{3}$$ Subtract these 2 equations. $$100x=83.\overline{3}$$ $$-10x=8.\overline{3}$$ $$\overline{90x=75}$$ Divide by 90 $$\frac{90x=75}{90}$$ $$x=5/6$$
22 PART B	D	Divide 8 into 5 and leave 4 in front of the decimal point.

Question No.	Answer	Detailed Explanation
23 PART A	B	Positive rate of change (slope) means a positive function and since it's an equation, it will be linear.
23 PART B	A	A slope between 0 and 1 will give us a less steep slope than the original equation.
24 PART A	A, B, C, D	Dilations change the size of a figure, but does not affect the similarity, the shape of the figure, and angle measures.
24 PART B	A, B, E	The two triangles cannot be congruent because of a dilation and angle AC'B doesn't exist.
25 PART A	C	4 squared is 16 and 5 squared is 25, which the square root of 20 will fall between nicely.
25 PART B	D	The decimal approximation will be a little less than half since the square root of 20 is less than half, which would be 4.4.
26	E	Decimals that never terminate or repeat are irrational numbers.
27	C	The simplified answer is $1/3^4 = 1/81$.
28 PART A	A	The way to find out the answer to a cube problem is to take the cube root of both sides.
28 PART B	B	The cube root of 343 is 7.
29	C, E	It shows a positive association along with a linear association.
30	A, C, D	It shows that nothing is going on and that there are points that are nowhere near the cluster of other points.
31	B, C	Scatterplot C shows a negative association and it also shows a linear relationship as well.
32	E	$2c+4f=82$ $9c+f=-22$ Multiply the second question by -4 $2c+4f=82$ $-36c-4f=88$ Combining these 2 equations we get $-34c=170$ Divide by -34 and we can get the Celsius temperature $c=-5$

LumosLearning.com   ◄

Question No.	Answer	Detailed Explanation
33	A	$2c+4f=82$

Plug -5 in for c so we can solve for Fahrenheit.

$2(-5)+4f=82$
$-10+4f=82$

Combine like terms

$4f=92$

Divide by 4 to solve for f

$f=23$

Notes

LumosLearning.com

End-Of-Year Assessment (EOY) - 2

Student Name:

Test Date:

Start Time:

End Time:

Here are some reminders for when you are taking the Grade 8 Mathematics End-of-Year Assessment (EOY).

To answer the questions on the test, use the directions given in the question. If you do not know the answer to a question, skip it and go on to the next question. If time permits, you may return to questions in this session only. Do your best to answer every question.

1. **PART A**

   Which of the following groupings is a function?

   Ⓐ {(1,3),(7,1),(8,10),(7,7) }
   Ⓑ {(0, 5), (0, 4), (0, 8), (0, 11)}
   Ⓒ {(1, 4), (3, 4), (7, 4), (1, 4)}
   Ⓓ {(2, 0), (-2, 7), (-9, 3), (-2, 9)}
   Ⓔ {(-7, 2), (-3, 4), (-1, 3), (0, 0)}

   PART B

   Which of the following is not a function?

   Ⓐ

x	1	2	4
y	3	3	3

   Ⓑ

x	2	4	6
y	4	5	6

	C		
x	3	4	5
y	2	5	8

	D		
x	0	0	0
y	-1	-2	-3

	E		
x	-7	-4	0
y	-7	-4	0

2. Which of the following functions are not linear. Choose all that apply

Ⓐ $a^2+b^2=c^2$

Ⓑ $y=3x+5$

Ⓒ $x=\dfrac{-b \pm \sqrt{b2 - 4ac}}{2a}$

Ⓓ $A=\pi r^2$

Ⓔ $\dfrac{3}{(x+1)}$

3. △ABC has points at the following coordinates: A (4, 9), B (-2, 3), and C (3, -4). Rotate the triangle 180° about the origin to form △A'B'C'.

PART A

What are the coordinates of A'?

Ⓐ (-4,-9)

Ⓑ (-4, 9)

Ⓒ (4, -9)

Ⓓ (-9, 4)

Ⓔ (9, -4)

PART B

What are the coordinates of B'?

(A) (-3, 2)
(B) (-3,-2)
(C) (3, -2)
(D) (-2, 3)
(E) (2, -3)

PART C

What are the coordinates of C'?

(A) (3, -4)
(B) (-3, 4)
(C) (-4, 3)
(D) (-3,-4)
(E) (-4,-3)

4. ## PART A

Tyrell is climbing Mt. Texas. The table below shows the distance he climbs each hour. He needs to be at the peak within 6 hours. The total climbing distance is 4 miles. Which equation below best describes the data?

Distance (hr)	$\frac{5}{8}$	$\frac{2}{3}$	$\frac{5}{8}$	$\frac{2}{3}$	$\frac{3}{8}$	$\frac{2}{3}$	$\frac{3}{8}$
Time (hr)	0	1	2	3	4	5	6

(A) $d = rt$

(B) $d = t$

(C) $d = \frac{2}{3}t$

(D) $d = \frac{1}{4}t$

(E) $d = \frac{7}{8}t$

PART B

If we use the equation from above, the rate of change, or slope, can be interpreted as meaning that an additional hour of climbing would give us _____ miles of distance. Which answer completes this sentence correctly?

(A) 1

(B) $\dfrac{1}{2}$

(C) $\dfrac{1}{4}$

(D) $\dfrac{2}{3}$

(E) no change

5.   A cone has a diameter of 8 cm and a height of 15 cm. What is the length of the slant height of the cone?

(A) $\dfrac{19}{2}$

(B) $\dfrac{241}{2}$

(C) $\sqrt{241}$

(D) $\dfrac{209}{2}$

(E) $\sqrt{209}$

6.   Which of the following is the correct decimal form of $\dfrac{7}{9}$?

(A) 0.7
(B) 0.77
(C) $0.\overline{7}$
(D) 0.78
(E) 0.778

7. **PART A**

Which of the following statements are true? There may be more than one correct answer.

Ⓐ Rational numbers can be natural, whole, and/or integers, but they are always real numbers.
Ⓑ All rational numbers can be written as decimals.
Ⓒ Rational numbers include decimals that don't terminate or repeat.
Ⓓ Irrational numbers can be written as terminating or repeating decimals
Ⓔ All irrational numbers are real numbers.

PART B

Which of the following are irrational numbers? There may be more than one answer.

Ⓐ $\sqrt{16}$

Ⓑ $\sqrt[3]{8}$

Ⓒ $\sqrt{17}$

Ⓓ π

Ⓔ $\sqrt{225}$

PART C

Which of the following fractions represents the decimal $1.\overline{09}$?

Ⓐ $\dfrac{7}{6}$

Ⓑ $\dfrac{10}{9}$

Ⓒ $\dfrac{4}{3}$

Ⓓ $\dfrac{11}{9}$

Ⓔ $\dfrac{12}{11}$

8. ΔABC has points at A (2, 4), B (3, 7), and C (4, 5). Dilate ΔABC by a scale factor of -2.5 forming ΔA' B' C'.

PART A

What are the coordinates of ΔA' B' C'?

Ⓐ A' (5,10),B' (7.5,17.5),C' (10,12.5)
Ⓑ A' (-5,-10),B' (-7.5,-17.5),C' (-10,-12.5)
Ⓒ A' (10,5),B' (7.5,17.5),C' (12.5,10)
Ⓓ A' (-10,-5),B' (-7.5,-17.5),C' (-12.5,-10)
Ⓔ A' (-4,-8),B' (-6,-14),C' (-8,-10)

PART B

Reflect ΔA'B'C' over the x-axis to form ΔA''B''C''. What are the coordinates of B''?

Ⓐ B'' (-7.5,17.5)
Ⓑ B'' (7.5,-17.5)
Ⓒ B'' (-6,14)
Ⓓ B'' (7.5,17.5)
Ⓔ B'' (-7.5,-17.5)

PART C

Reflect ΔA''B''C'' over the y-axis to form ΔA'''B'''C'''. What are the coordinates of A'''?

Ⓐ A''' (-5,-10)
Ⓑ A''' (5,-10)
Ⓒ A''' (5,10)
Ⓓ A''' (-5,10)
Ⓔ A''' (10,-5)

LumosLearning.com   ▶

Translate ΔA'''B'''C''' 5 units left and 7 units up. What are the new coordinates of ΔA''''B''''C''''?

Ⓐ A'''' (0,17) B'''' (-2.5,24.5) C''''(-5,19.5)
Ⓑ A'''' (0,-17) B'''' (-2.5,-24.5) C'''' (-5,-19.5)
Ⓒ A'''' (0,-17) B'''' (2.5,-24.5) C'''' (5,-19.5)
Ⓓ A'''' (0,17) B'''' (2.5,24.5) C'''' (5,19.5)
Ⓔ A'''' (17,0) B'''' (24.5,2.5) C''''(19.5,5)

9. What is $0.\overline{6}$ written as a fraction in lowest terms?

Ⓐ $\dfrac{1}{3}$

Ⓑ $\dfrac{1}{6}$

Ⓒ $\dfrac{1}{9}$

Ⓓ $\dfrac{5}{6}$

Ⓔ $\dfrac{2}{3}$

10. What is $1.\overline{23}$ written as a fraction in lowest terms?

Ⓐ $1\dfrac{2}{3}$

Ⓑ $1\dfrac{23}{100}$

Ⓒ $1\dfrac{23}{99}$

Ⓓ $1\dfrac{2}{9}$

Ⓔ $1\dfrac{22}{99}$

11. PART A

Between which two numbers would the √33 fall?

- Ⓐ 3 and 4
- Ⓑ 4 and 5
- Ⓒ 5 and 6
- Ⓓ 6 and 7
- Ⓔ 7 and 8

PART B

Which number would it be closer to?

- Ⓐ 3
- Ⓑ 4
- Ⓒ 5
- Ⓓ 6
- Ⓔ 7

PART C

How do you know which number it would be closer to?

- Ⓐ The √33 is closer to the √49 so it will be closer to 7.
- Ⓑ The √33 is closer to the √36 so it will be closer to 6.
- Ⓒ The √33 is closer to the √25 so it will be closer to 5
- Ⓓ The √33 is closer to the √16 so it will be closer to 4
- Ⓔ The √33 is closer to the √9 so it will be closer to 3

12. **PART A**

If $x^3 = 512$, which of the following answer choices is a solution for x? There may be more than one correct answer.

Ⓐ x = 8
Ⓑ x = 170.$\overline{6}$
Ⓒ x = 256
Ⓓ x = -8
Ⓔ x = -256

PART B

If the answer to an equation is the x=-5, what could have the equation been? Select all that apply.

Ⓐ $x^2 = 25$

Ⓑ $x^2 = -25$

Ⓒ $x = \sqrt[3]{125}$

Ⓓ $x = -\sqrt[3]{125}$

Ⓔ $2x+3 = -7$

13. Which of the following expressions are equivalent to 49? Select all that apply.

Ⓐ 7×2

Ⓑ 7^2

Ⓒ $\dfrac{1}{7^{-2}}$

Ⓓ $\dfrac{1}{-7}$

Ⓔ $7^{-1}(7^4)(7^{-5})(7^0)$

14. ΔABC has coordinates at A (0,3),B (5,2),and C (3,4). ΔA''B''C'' has coordinates at A'' (0,-6),B'' (10,-4),C'' (6,-8). Choose an answer below that describes the transformation from ΔABC to ΔA''B''C''.

    Ⓐ   ΔA''B''C'' is a dilation of ΔABC

    Ⓑ   ΔA''B''C'' is a reflection of ΔABC

    Ⓒ   ΔA''B''C'' is a translation of ΔABC

    Ⓓ   ΔA''B''C'' is a rotation of ΔABC

    Ⓔ   ΔA''B''C'' is a dilation of ΔA'B'C', which was formed by a reflection of ΔABC.

15. Draw ΔABC. Extend $\overrightarrow{AC}$ outside the triangle and label point P on this ray. Let ∠A be ∠1, ∠B be ∠2, ∠C be ∠3, and ∠PCB be ∠4.

PART A

Which of the following statements are true? There may be more than one correct answer.

    Ⓐ   m∠1+m∠2+m∠3=180°

    Ⓑ   m∠3+m∠4=180°

    Ⓒ   m∠3=m∠4

    Ⓓ   m∠1+m∠2+m∠3=m∠3+m∠4

    Ⓔ   m∠1+m∠2=m∠4

PART B

Draw $\overleftrightarrow{FG}$ through B so it's || to $\overline{AC}$. Which of the following statements below are true? There may be more than one correct answer.

    Ⓐ   ∠GBC + ∠PCB = 180°

    Ⓑ   ∠BAC = ∠ACB

    Ⓒ   ∠FBC = ∠4

    Ⓓ   ∠2 = ∠4

    Ⓔ   ∠3 = ∠CBG

16. The 8th grade class has 90 students. Out of the 90 students, 45 are in drama. 20 of the drama students are also in choir.

PART A

Which ratio below represents the number of drama students to the drama students that are also in choir?

Ⓐ $\frac{45}{20}$

Ⓑ $\frac{9}{4}$

Ⓒ $\frac{4}{9}$

Ⓓ $\frac{1}{2}$

Ⓔ $\frac{2}{9}$

PART B

Which ratio shows the number of students not in drama and choir compared to the total number of students?

Ⓐ $\frac{9}{5}$

Ⓑ $\frac{5}{9}$

Ⓒ $\frac{1}{2}$

Ⓓ $\frac{5}{14}$

Ⓔ $\frac{14}{5}$

17. Which of the following translations keeps angle measurements congruent to the original figure? There may be more than one answer.

    (A) Reflection
    (B) Rotation
    (C) Dilation
    (D) Translation
    (E) None of the above

18. Which of the following can we use to determine if a data set represents a function? There may be more than one answer.

    (A) Vertical line test
    (B) Make sure "y" values do not repeat
    (C) Make sure there is one and only one input for each output
    (D) Make sure each x-value has more than one y-value
    (E) Make a table to determine the numbers in the domain appear only once.

19. ΔABC has coordinates at A (4,2), B (-3,-9), C (3,-2).

    ### PART A

    After translating ΔABC 7 units left and 5 units down, which of the following statements are true? There may be more than one.

    (A) ΔA'B'C' is located in Quadrant III
    (B) ΔABC ≅ ΔA'B'C'
    (C) m ∠B is <m ∠B'
    (D) The coordinates of B' are (4,-4)
    (E) m ∠A ≅ m ∠B'

    ### PART B

    Now reflect ΔA'B'C' over the y-axis to form ΔA''B''C''. Which of the following are true? Select all that may apply.

    (A) ΔA'' B''C'' is located in Quadrant IV
    (B) ΔA'' B''C'' is bigger than ΔA'B'C'
    (C) ΔA'' B''C'' is smaller than ΔABC
    (D) ΔA''B''C'' is located in Quadrant II
    (E) ΔA'' B''C'' is the same size as ΔA'B'C'

          ▶

PART C

Rotate ΔA''B''C'' 90° counterclockwise forming ΔA'''B'''C'''. Which of the following statements are true. Select all that may apply.

Ⓐ All coordinates for ΔA'''B'''C''' are positive
Ⓑ All coordinates for ΔA'''B'''C''' are negative
Ⓒ ΔA'''B'''C''' falls in Quadrant III
Ⓓ ΔA'''B'''C''' falls in Quadrant I
Ⓔ ΔA'''B'''C''' is bigger than ΔA'B'C

PART D

Dilate ΔA'''B'''C''' by a scale factor of $-\dfrac{3}{4}$. Which of the following is not true?

Ⓐ ΔA'''' B'''' C'''' is smaller than ΔA''' B''' C'''.
Ⓑ The angles of ΔA'''' B'''' C'''' ≅ ΔA''' B''' C'''.
Ⓒ ΔA'''' B'''' C'''' is the same size as ΔA''' B''' C'''.
Ⓓ The sides of ΔA'''' B'''' C'''' are proportional to ΔA' B' C'.
Ⓔ ΔA'''' B'''' C'''' will be upside down when graphed.

20. Which of the following statements is true?

Ⓐ A number is called irrational if it has a decimal that repeats.
Ⓑ A number is called irrational if it is a perfect square.
Ⓒ A number is called irrational if it has a decimal that terminates.
Ⓓ A number is called irrational if we can write it as a fraction.
Ⓔ None of the above.

21.

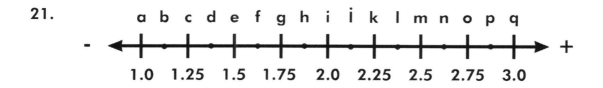

Which of the following points on the number line is the best estimate of √2?

Ⓐ a
Ⓑ b
Ⓒ c
Ⓓ d
Ⓔ e

22. The diameter of the nucleus of a helium atom is 3.8×10^{-15}. What is this number expressed in standard notation?

Ⓐ 0.0000000000038
Ⓑ 0.00000000000038
Ⓒ 0.0000000000000038
Ⓓ 0.00000000000000038
Ⓔ 0.000000000000000038

23. The average diameter of the planet Jupiter is 86,881 miles. The average diameter of the Earth is 7.9×10^3.

PART A

About how many times bigger is the diameter of Jupiter than the Earth?

Ⓐ About 11 times.
Ⓑ About 12 times.
Ⓒ About 13 times.
Ⓓ About 14 times.
Ⓔ About 15 times.

PART B

Saturn has a diameter of about 7.2×10^4 miles. About how many times bigger is the diameter of Saturn than that of the Earth?

Ⓐ About 5 times.
Ⓑ About 6 times.
Ⓒ About 7 times.
Ⓓ About 8 times.
Ⓔ About 9 times.

LumosLearning.com ▶

24. Eric traveled 4500 miles across the country to visit his parents. On day 1, he traveled 875 miles. On day 2 and 3, he traveled 950 miles each day. On day 4, he traveled 750 miles. On the last day, he traveled the remaining 975 miles. Which of the following would describe this data if it were made into a scatterplot?

   Ⓐ Clustering
   Ⓑ Outliers
   Ⓒ Non-linear relationship
   Ⓓ Positive linear relationship
   Ⓔ Negative linear Relationship

25. Which of the following is the correct solution to $x^2=64$?

   Ⓐ 32
   Ⓑ ±8
   Ⓒ ±16
   Ⓓ 4
   Ⓔ -4

26. Emily calculated the volume of a cylinder to be 432π ft³. Which shape below would have the same   volume as the cone?

   Ⓐ A cube with a side length of 4π inches
   Ⓑ A triangle that has a base of 96 inches2 and a height of 9π inches.
   Ⓒ A cone with a radius of 16π inches
   Ⓓ A rectangular prism with a length of 7 inches, a width of 13 inches, and a height of 11π inches.
   Ⓔ A sphere with a radius of 6 inches.

27. Marisa found the volume of a sphere to be $\dfrac{256\pi}{3}$ in³. Which of the following answers could be the length of the radius of the sphere?

   Ⓐ 2 inches
   Ⓑ 3 inches
   Ⓒ 4 inches
   Ⓓ 5 inches
   Ⓔ 6 inches

28. Which metric measurement would be the most accurate when measuring the length of the diameter of a quarter?

  Ⓐ Millimeters
  Ⓑ Centimeters
  Ⓒ Meters
  Ⓓ Decameters
  Ⓔ Kilometers

29. Which of the following expressions can be used to represent the number 5? There may be more than one correct answer.

  Ⓐ $5^3 \times 5^{-2}$

  Ⓑ $\dfrac{5^7}{5^6}$

  Ⓒ $5^7 \times 5^0 \times 5^{-6}$

  Ⓓ $\dfrac{5^{-18}}{5^{-14}}$

  Ⓔ None of the above

30. Which of the following transformations will not affect parallel lines?

  Ⓐ Dilation
  Ⓑ Translation
  Ⓒ Reflection
  Ⓓ Rotation
  Ⓔ None of the above

31. Which of the following transformations will cause line segments to be proportional

  Ⓐ Dilation
  Ⓑ Translation
  Ⓒ Reflection
  Ⓓ Rotation
  Ⓔ None of the above

LumosLearning.com

32.   Which two numbers below will give us the best estimate of √7?

   (A) 2.6 and 2.7
   (B) 2.64 and 2.65
   (C) 2.645 and 2.646
   (D) 2.6457 and 2.6458
   (E) 2.64575 and 2.65576

33. $\overline{AB}$ has coordinates of A (3,2),and B (7,9). It is rotated 180° about the origin. Which of the following is true about $\overline{A' B'}$? There may be more than one answer.

   (A) $\overline{A' B'}$ is the same length as $\overline{AB}$.
   (B) A' is located at (3,-2)
   (C) B' is located at (-7,-9)
   (D) A' B' is a line segment
   (E) A' B' is longer than $\overline{AB}$.

End of End-Of-Year Assessment (EOY) - 2

End-Of-Year Assessment (EOY) - 2

Answer Key

Question No.	Answer	Related Lumos Online Workbook	CCSS
1 PART A	E	Functions	8.F.1
1 PART B	D	Functions	8.F.1
2	A, C, D, E	Linear Functions	8.F.3
3 PART A	A	Analyzing Transformations	8.G.3
3 PART B	E	Analyzing Transformations	8.G.3
3 PART C	B	Analyzing Transformations	8.G.3
4 PART A	C	Analyzing Linear Scatterplots	8.SP.3
4 PART B	D	Analyzing Linear Scatterplots	8.SP.3
5	E	Pythagorean Theorem in Real-World Problems	8.G.7
6	C	Rational Vs. Irrational Numbers	8.NS.1
7 PART A	A, B, E	Rational Vs. Irrational Numbers	8.NS.1
7 PART B	C, D	Rational Vs. Irrational Numbers	8.NS.1
7 PART C	E	Rational Vs. Irrational Numbers	8.NS.1
8 PART A	B	Analyzing Transformations	8.G.3
8 PART B	A	Analyzing Transformations	8.G.3
8 PART C	C	Analyzing Transformations	8.G.3
8 PART D	D	Analyzing Transformations	8.G.3
9	E	Rational Vs. Irrational Numbers	8.NS.1
10	C	Rational Vs. Irrational Numbers	8.NS.1
11 PART A	C	Approximating Irrational Numbers	8.NS.2
11 PART B	D	Approximating Irrational Numbers	8.NS.2
11 PART C	B	Approximating Irrational Numbers	8.NS.2
12 PART A	A	Square and Cube Roots	8.EE.2
12 PART B	A, B, D, E	Square and Cube Roots	8.EE.2
13	B,C	Properties of Exponents	8.EE.1
14	E	Transformations and Similarity	8.G.4
15 Part A	A, B, D, E	Interior and Exterior Angles in Geometric Figures	8.G.5
15 PART B	A, C, E	Rational vs. Irrational Numbers	8.NS.1
16 PART A	B	Relatable Data Frequency	8.SP.4

LumosLearning.com   ▶

Question No.	Answer	Related Lumos Online Workbook	CCSS
16 PART B	D	Relatable Data Frequency	8.SP.4
17	A, B, C, D	Transformations of Points and Lines	8.G.1
18	A, C, E	Linear Functions	8.F.3
19 PART A	A, B	Transformations of Points and Lines Analyzing Transformations	8.G.1 8.G.3
19 PART B	D, E	Transformations of Points and Lines Analyzing Transformations	8.G.1 8.G.3
19 PART C	A, D	Transformations of Points and Lines Analyzing Transformations	8.G.1 8.G.3
19 PART D	C, E	Transformations of Points and Lines Analyzing Transformations	8.G.1 8.G.3
20	E	Rational vs. Irrational Numbers	8.NS.1
21	E	Approximating Irrational Numbers	8.NS.2
22	C	Scientific Notation	8.EE.3
23 PART A	A	Scientific Notation	8.EE.3
23 PART B	E	Scientific Notation	8.EE.3
24	D	Scientific Notation	8.EE.3
25	A	Scatterplots, Lines of Best Fit	8.SP.2
26	B	Finding Volume: Cone, Cylinder, and Sphere	8.G.9
27	C	Square and Cube Roots	8.EE.2
28	A	Solving Problems Involving Scientific Notation	8.EE.4
29	A, B, C, D	Properties of Exponents	8.EE.1
30	A, B, C, D	Transformations of Points and Lines	8.G.1
31	A	Analyzing Transformations	8.G.3
32	E	Approximating Irrational Numbers	8.NS.2
33	A, D	Transformations of Points and Lines	8.G.1

End-Of-Year Assessment (EOY) - 2

Detailed Explanations

Question No.	Answer	Detailed Explanation
1 PART A	E	Functions have x-values that do not repeat.
1 PART B	D	Functions have x-values that do not repeat.
2	A, C, D, E	Linear functions do not have exponents or variables in the denominator.
3 PART A	A	When rotating counterclockwise about the origin, you make the y-value negative and switch the x and y values.
3 PART B	E	When rotating counterclockwise about the origin, you make the y-value negative and switch the x and y values
3 PART C	B	When rotating counterclockwise about the origin, you make the y-value negative and switch the x and y values
4 PART A	C	When looking at how much distance is covered per hour, most of the values are around 2/3.
4 PART B	D	Each hour, we gain 2/3 miles.
5	E	Using the Pythagorean theorem, we can find the missing value. The radius of 4 cm is "a", the height of 15 cm is "b", and the slant height is the hypotenuse or side "c".
6	C	Dividing 9 into 7 will give us the correct answer.
7 PART A	A, B, E	C describes irrational numbers and D describes rational numbers.
7 PART B	C, D	Irrational numbers don't terminate or repeat. C and D are the only ones that do that.
7 PART C	E	let $100x = 109.\overline{09}$ let $x = 1.\overline{09}$ $99x = 108$ $\dfrac{96x = 108}{99}$ $x = \dfrac{108}{9}$ $x = \dfrac{12}{11}$
8 PART A	B	Take each coordinate times -2.5 to get the new coordinates.

 LumosLearning.com ▶

Question No.	Answer	Detailed Explanation
8 PART B	A	Reflecting over the x-axis causes the y-values to become their opposites
8 PART C	C	When reflecting over the y-axis, the x-values become their opposites.
8 PART D	D	Move each coordinate 5 units left then 7 units up.
9	E	let $10x = 6.\overline{6}$ let $x = 0.\overline{6}$ $9x = 6$ $\dfrac{9x = 6}{9}$ $X = \dfrac{6}{9}$ $x = \dfrac{2}{3}$
10	C	let $100x = 123.\overline{23}$ let $x = 1.\overline{23}$ $99x = 122$ $\dfrac{99X = 122}{99}$ $x = \dfrac{122}{99}$ $x = 1\dfrac{23}{99}$
11 PART A	C	The square root of 33 will be between 5 and 6.
11 PART B	D	It will be closer to 6.
11 PART C	B	Letter B gives the correct explanation.
12 PART A	A	8 times 8 times 8 gives us 512, which is the only answer that works for this problem.
12 PART B	A, D, E	Substitute the value of -5 in for x in each problem. Only B and C don't work.
13	B, C	7 times 7 will give us 49. In answer C, because the exponent is negative, to make it positive, we write the reciprocal. It will also be 7 times 7, which gives us 49.

Question No.	Answer	Detailed Explanation
14	E	The only way that the transformation will be able to happen is if there is a combination of transformations. None of them alone have the power to move the triangle from ABC to A''B''C''.
15 PART A	A, B, D, E	The sum of the two nonadjacent interior angles equals the exterior angle of a triangle. The only thing that isn't true is that angle 3 is not equal to angle 4.
15 PART B	A, C, E	A—Consecutive Interior Angles add up to 180, C—Alternate Interior Angles, E—Alternate Interior Angles
16 PART A	B	$\frac{45}{20}$, which simplifies to $\frac{9}{5}$
16 PART B	D	$\frac{25}{90}$, which simplifies to $\frac{5}{14}$
17	A, B, C, D	All of the transformations will keep angle measurements congruent
18	A, C, E	Vertical line test allows the line to touch a graph only once if it's linear, one input (x) for each output (y), and domain values (x) can only show up once.
19 PART A	A, B	Following the translation will put the triangle clearly in Quadrant III and the two triangles are congruent.
19 PART B	D,E	The reflection will put the new triangle in quadrant 2 and it will be the same size as the original.
19 PART C	A, D	All of the values after the rotation will be positive and means that the triangle is in quadrant I.
19 PART D	C	All of them are true except for C because a dilation changes the size.
20	E	None of those statements are true. If you were to switch the word irrational to rational, then all 4 statements would be true.
21	E	The square root of 2 is between 1 and 2. It's closest approximation is 1.5.
22	C	Since the exponent is -15, that means 15 moves left. It will take us one move to get in front of the 3, which means we need to add 14 zeros.
23 PART A	A	Put Jupiter into scientific notation, which is about 8.7×10^5 and divide that by earth's diameter. It gives us about 11 times.
23 PART B	E	Comparing the diameter of Earth to Saturn gives us about 9 times as big for the diameter of Saturn than the Earth.
24	D	Plotting this data will give us a positive linear relationship.
25	A	The square root of 64 is both positive and negative 8.

Question No.	Answer	Detailed Explanation
26	B	Calculating the volume of the various shapes, the only one that will give us the same volume of a cylinder is the volume of the triangular prism.
27	C	Working backwards using the formula for the volume of a sphere, the only radius length that makes the volume true is 4.
28	A	The best distance to measure the diameter of a quarter is the millimeter.
29	A, B, C, D	5^1 is the same thing as 5. Following our exponent rules all answers except E will give us an answer of 5.
30	A, B, C, D	Not affecting parallel lines is something all transformations do.
31	A	Proportionality is caused by dilations.
32	E	The further we can go out on the estimation, the closer it will be to the real approximation.
33	A, D	When rotating 180 degrees around the origin, will not change the fact that it's a line segment, nor will it change its length.

Notes

     LumosLearning.com   ▶

Notes

Lumos StepUp™ is an educational App that helps students learn and master grade-level skills in Math and English Language Arts.

The list of features includes:

- Learn Anywhere, Anytime!

- Grades 3-8 Mathematics and English Language Arts

- Get instant access to the Common Core State Standards

- One full-length sample practice test in all Grades and Subjects

- Full-length Practice Tests, Partial Tests and Standards-based Tests

- 2 Test Modes: Normal mode and Learning mode

- Learning Mode gives the user a step-by-step explanation if the answer is wrong

- Access to Online Workbooks

- Provides ability to directly scan QR Codes

- And it's completely FREE!

http://lumoslearning.com/a/stepup-app

About Online Workbooks

- ◆ When you buy this book, 1 year access to online workbooks included

- ◆ Access them anytime from a computer with an internet connection

- ◆ Adheres to the New Common Core State Standards

- ◆ Includes progress reports

- ◆ Instant feedback and self-paced

- ◆ Ability to review incorrect answers

- ◆ Parents and Teachers can assist in student's learning by reviewing their areas of difficulty

Course Name: Grade 4 Math Prep

Lesson Name:	Correct	Total	% Score	Incorrect
Introduction				
Diagnostic Test		3	0%	3
Number and Numerical Operations				
Workbook - Number Sense	2	10	20%	8
Workbook - Numerical Operations	2	25	8%	23
Workbook - Estimation	1	3	33%	2
Geometry and measurement				
Workbook - Geometric Properties		6	0%	6
Workbook - Transforming Shapes				
Workbook - Coordinate Geometry	1	3	33%	2
Workbook - Units of Measurement				
Workbook - Measuring Geometric Objects	3	10	30%	7
Patterns and algebra				
Workbook - Patterns	7	10	70%	3
Workbook - Functions and relationships				

LESSON NAME: Workbook - Geometric Properties

Elapsed Time: 01:19

Question No. 2

What type of motion is being modeled here?

Select right answer
- ◯ a translation
- ◯ a rotation 90° clockwise
- ◉ a rotation 90° counter-clockwise
- ◯ a reflection

[Previous question]   [Next question]

Report Name: Missed Questions

Student Name: Lisa Colbright
Cours Name: Grade 4 Math Prep
Lesson Name: Diagnostic Test

The faces on a number cube are labeled with the numbers 1 through 6. What is the probability of rolling a number greater than 4?

Answer Explanation

(C) On a standard number cube, there are six possible outcomes. Of those outcomes, 2 of them are greater than 4. Thus, the probability of rolling a number greater than 4 is "2 out of 6" or 2/6.

A)   1/6
B)   1/3
C) Correct Answer   2/6
D)   3/6

Made in the USA
Middletown, DE
04 January 2015